Business Checklists

Small Business Management

Orders; please contact Bookpoint Ltd, 78 Milton Park, Abingdon, Oxon OX14 4TD. Telephone: (44) 01235 400414, Fax: (44) 01235 400454. Lines are open from 9.00–6.00, Monday to Saturday, with a 24 hour message answering service. Email address: orders@bookpoint.co.uk

British Library Cataloguing in Publication Data
A catalogue record for this title is available from the British Library

ISBN 0 340 74293 3

RBL
658.022

First published 1999
Impression number   10 9 8 7 6 5 4 3 2 1
Year   2005 2004 2003 2002 2001 2000 1999

Typeset by GreenGate Publishing Services, Tonbridge, Kent.
Printed in Great Britain for Hodder and Stoughton Educational, a division of Hodder Headline Plc, 338 Euston Road, London NW1 3BH, by Redwood Books, Trowbridge, Wiltshire

Contents

iu *the Institute*
of Management

F O U N D A T I O N

The mission of the Institute of Management (IM) is to promote the art and science of management.

The Instititue embraces all levels of management from student to chief executive and supports its own Foundation which provides a unique portfolio of services for all managers, enabling them to develop skills and achieve management excellence.

For information on the various levels and benefits of membership, please contact:

Department HS
Institute of Management
Cottingham Road
Corby
Northants NN17 1TT
Tel: 01536 204222
Fax: 01536 201651

Preface

The first Business Checklists were launched by the Institute of Management in 1995. They met with immediate success from managers in all sectors of commerce and industry, and in organisations of all shapes and sizes.

They originated from one simple idea – that managers did not have the time, or indeed the inclination, to plough through heavy tomes of turgid prose in order to unearth the odd nugget or two which might enable them to do their jobs a little better. They also drew their origins from a former series of Checklists by the British Institute of Management which had been successful in the 1970s.

So why are they so successful? Basically because they cut out unnecessary waffle. They express in clear, concise language what managers need to know, and are presented in a consistent format so that it is easy to pick out the bits you want. They have a wide application, outside business as well as inside, and in small or large organisations: introducing a concept or technique, explaining the pros and cons, dos and don'ts, and steps to follow to get you started. They also provide further pointers for those who do have the time, inclination or need to pursue the topic in greater depth.

Updated and revised since their launch, the Business Checklists are here presented for the first time in a series of books which bring them together under broad management functions.

How are the subjects chosen? Not by guesswork or experts who think they know best, but by demand. The Institute's Management Information Centre handles over 50,000 enquiries a year so the Centre's researchers not only have a good idea of what managers are looking for but also how they want it delivered.

Each checklist follows a similar pattern:

MCI Standards

The MCI Management Standards are the underpinning structure for many vocational management qualifications. Each checklist identifies the appropriate subject content of the standards that it meets.

Definition

Clarifies the coverage of the checklist, highlighting both what is and what is not included in its scope.

Advantages and disadvantages

Each checklist highlights the benefits and pitfalls of the topic, providing a quick insight into the experiences of others.

Action checklist

The core of the checklist is the step-by-step sequence, written in jargon-free language and designed to help readers get to grips with a task quickly.

Dos and don'ts

A brief summary of the key items to remember – and to avoid – on each topic.

Useful reading and organisations

Sources of additional information for readers wishing to investigate the topic further.

Thought starters

Some introductory ideas to help readers begin to approach the subject in a practical way.

Although the Business Checklists constitute a wide-ranging, but concise, library of management know-how, we don't pretend – yet – that they are complete. As they are being continually updated and revised, please get in touch with the Institute of Management's Information Centre in Corby if you have suggestions for future editions.

Bob Norton
Head of Information Services
Institute of Management.

Starting a Small Business

This checklist is designed to help those who are considering setting up their own business.

MCI Standards

This checklist has relevance for the MCI Management Standards: Key Roles A and B – Manage Activities and Manage Resources.

Definition

There are many definitions of a 'small business'. They are more relevant to business statisticians than to would-be entrepreneurs. Anyone who is starting a business will be involved in a small business. By the time the size of the business reaches any of the dimensions commonly used – such as number of employees, turnover, or balance sheet total – the owner's problems will not be those of starting a business, but those of sustaining its existence and growth.

However, over 96% of businesses in the United Kingdom have a turnover of less than £1 million and 93% of all businesses employ fewer than 10 people. These figures should offer would-be entrepreneurs some encouragement – they will not be alone.

Benefits of starting your own business

Benefits include:

- having control over what you do and how you do it
- achieving self-determination as your 'own boss'
- gaining independence and freedom from the authority of others
- enjoying the satisfaction of making a success of your own endeavours
- using your energy to promote your interests – not those of others.

Drawbacks of starting your own business

- You will be taking risks with your own, or borrowed, capital.
- You will be working long hours.
- The responsibility of success or failure, and for the welfare of those you may employ, will rest with you and you alone.
- All the functions of the business, such as accounting and VAT, become your responsibility – 'Accounts', 'Marketing', 'Planning' and 'Personnel' are all you.
- You will not enjoy the security of paid employment.

Action checklist

1. Consider why you want to be self-employed

Ask yourself:

- why you want to change your status
- if you should be seeking (alternative) paid employment
- if you want to work long, perhaps lonely, hours
- if you have the support of your family or partner
- if they understand the risks you will be taking
- if you will be able to work at and from home, if necessary
- which skills you have that may add value to products or services
- if you have the stamina to keep going in the face of difficulties
- if friends and associates regard you as resilient
- if you enjoy good health
- if you really do have something to offer which people will pay for.

2. List your assets and liabilities

Your business will require capital. Whether you can afford it with or without borrowing will depend on your existing assets. What is the value of your house, life assurance policies, material possessions, shares, savings or any other assets? Similarly, what is the extent of your financial commitments over the next 3–5 years? Have you considered everything? What overheads do you need to cover and what liabilities need to be accounted for? Can your assets be turned into cash? How much cash can you put on the table? Talk it over with your bank manager even at this preliminary stage.

3. Ask yourself what you want to get out of your own business

What are you really looking for? Freedom? Fortune? A chance to leave the City behind? Opportunities to travel, to meet people, or to develop a 'pet idea'? Less responsibility? Are your motives positive, ie to achieve something, or negative, ie to get away from something? Set your requirements down on paper, and be realistic. Are you really likely to achieve them, or are you 'pipe-dreaming'? Discuss all this with a friend.

4. Consider what type of products or services you intend to deliver

The clearer your focus, the sooner you will be able to start detailed planning. If you don't have a clear idea, the following pointers may help:

- Be cautious about becoming 'a consultant'. Do you have the necessary expertise? Don't be misled by books purporting to tell you how to make a fortune at it.
- Find out if there are any local opportunities in tourism or leisure.
- Identify what goods and services large companies, local authorities and other public bodies buy in from outside the area.
- Research the possibility of selling goods made by others.
- Consider how you could improve on someone else's ideas, or go into partnership with them. If you try this approach alone, beware of the law of patents.
- Monitor the local newspapers – opportunities arise from the most unexpected and unusual situations.
- Check changes in legislation which might offer business opportunities of which you may be able to take advantage.
- Consider advertising – anonymously – your availability to invest in, and share in the management of, a small business which is undercapitalised.

5. Investigate the market for your product or service

- What is your product or service?
- What unusual goods and services are required locally?
- Who will buy your product or service?
- Why should they buy yours and not someone else's?
- How many people will buy your product or service?
- Is it unique or are there many like it?
- Is the market stable, growing or shrinking?
- How many competitors would you have?
- How price-sensitive are products and services like yours?

6. Decide the ideal status of the business you wish to start

You may wish to become a **Sole Trader** operating alone and responsible for all aspects of the business, including all taxes, debts, and day-to-day running of the business.

An alternative is to enter into a **Partnership**, combining the skills and experience of two or more people. Work loads can be shared and operations can be managed more flexibly. Beware of inviting 'friends' to join you in a proposed partnership, for friendship's sake. Would they make good businessmen? Do you respect their judgement? What would they 'bring to the party'?

Look for a partner whose strengths complement yours. Business relationships depend upon a balance of skills. Satisfy yourself – and your proposed partner – that you are compatible.

Franchising is an increasingly popular and easy way of getting into your own business. You invest in a new 'branch' of a business already established. You will get considerable support from the initiator of the business with all the advantages of a proven product or service, but the rewards are limited by the franchise agreement. Make thorough enquiries about any franchise before committing yourself to a contract. See Useful addresses for possible sources of advice.

Establishing a **Limited Company** will restrict your liability but you are strongly advised to consult a solicitor or an accountant before taking this step. Satisfy yourself that the advantages outweigh the disadvantages.

Networking with business associates is an informal approach to levering advantage. Your business remains under your control but you build relationships with others in the same kind of business to share the costs of marketing and perhaps of delivery. This approach has no legal foundation, unless you enter into specific contracts with associates. It depends upon the trust you build up with your associates. Networking can lead to a wider range of customers and to the growth of your business. You must be prepared, however, to give, as well as to take.

7. Check your ability to cope with the pressures of running a business

Measure yourself against the following criteria (preferably on a scale of 1–5):

- I am self-disciplined.
- I do not let things drift.
- I have the full support of my family.
- I can cope under pressure.
- I am ready to put in seven days a week if necessary.
- I get on well with people and I can motivate them.
- I can make quick decisions when they are needed.
- I persist when the going gets tough.
- I can learn from mistakes and I can take advice.
- I am patient and I don't expect quick results.
- I am in good health, enthusiastic and aware of the risks.
- I have specific aims, including the need to look after myself and my family.

If you do not score well on these criteria (a score of at least 3 on every item), take another look at your reasons for wanting to set up your own business.

8. Draw up a business plan

The major banks provide advice on drawing up business plans. Consult more than one local branch to see what they can offer. Whether or not you need bank funding, you need a business plan and you can only benefit from a banker's views on the plan which you produce.

Dos and don'ts for starting a small business

Do
- Talk to others who have succeeded but made mistakes before you.
- Look at what start-up help is available.
- Consult an accountant and lawyer before committing yourself irrevocably.
- Prepare a business plan in consultation with your bank.

Don't
- Make any important decisions until you have talked them through with family, friends, advisers, and those who have 'been there already'.
- Try to set up a business just because it 'looks like a good idea'.
- Overstretch your financial resources – borrowed money has to be repaid, usually with interest.

Useful reading
Starting up, 3rd ed, Gary Jones, London: Pitman, 1995
Lloyds Bank small business guide, Sara Williams, London: Penguin Books, 1995
Starting your own business, Rev ed, London: Consumers Association, 1994
Working for yourself: the Daily Telegraph guide to self-employment, 15th ed, Godfrey Golzen, London: Kogan Page, 1994

Useful addresses
British Franchise Association Ltd., Thames View, Newtown Road, Henley-on-Thames, Oxon RG9 1HG, Tel: 01491 578049/50
Franchisee Association, 2 Moor Street, Ormskirk, Lancashire L39 2XN, Tel: 01695 574339

Thought starters

- What skills and experience do I have that will help me in my business?
- What are my financial commitments, at least for the next 3-5 years?
- How realistic am I being?

Running a Small Business from Home

This checklist is concerned with small business owners who operate their own businesses from home.

MCI Standards

This checklist has relevance for the MCI Management Standards: Key Roles A and B – Manage Activities and Manage Resources.

Definition

'A home-based business means working for yourself at home, all day, or part of the day, using your own home as a workbase.' (Baker)

A home-based business may use new communications technology to stay in touch with customers and suppliers. The business may buy in goods and services which are more efficiently produced by others.

Success depends on self-motivation and on sound planning and preparation.

Advantages of running your business from home

Running your business from home:

- produces cost savings by eliminating the overhead of separate premises
- has low start-up costs – there is no investment in additional real estate or rent
- saves time – there is no commuting to another location
- may result in some tax relief
- means you can work at the time of day best suited to you
- gives you peace and quiet – you have control of your working environment.

Disadvantages of running your business from home

It can mean:

- part of your home ceases to be available for usual domestic purposes
- interruptions – until family and friends realise that you are working
- distractions – and the difficulty of balancing your home life with work
- scheduling unattractive tasks, such as paperwork and administration, at times when home life offers more attractive diversions
- neighbours may see your business as a nuisance, especially if you have regular deliveries of goods or frequent visitors, or use noisy machinery in a workshop.

Action checklist

1. Find out about the law

Consult your legal adviser on your proposed business plan, and especially about how you wish to use your home as a base. There may be existing byelaws which could affect your intention to run your business from home. Your legal adviser will also ensure that any lease or tenancy agreement to which you are a party does not contain restrictions on business activities. Likewise, if you are a freeholder, you must seek advice on the contents of your title deeds and mortgage agreement. Some housing estates are subject to planning conditions which prohibit running a business from home and some mortgage contracts prevent the use of the home for a business. Council tenants must notify the council and follow its advice.

2. Check your insurance cover

Your buildings and contents insurance will probably be affected, so make sure you notify the insurance company of your plans and obtain adequate insurance cover.

Consult your legal adviser about professional indemnity insurance – mistakes can be costly and can damage your business reputation if you cannot resolve the complaints or problems of a dissatisfied customer.

Consider insurance to cover you if you cannot work for a long period of time. Without insurance, it is likely that you will lose income and put the business at risk.

3. Establish your tax position

Talk to your accountant about this – you may be able to set an amount for the 'business use' of your home against the profits of your business, before tax.

Beware of making excessive claims for the business use of the house; you may become liable for Capital Gains Tax on some of the proceeds of any subsequent sale of your house.

4. Choose your working area carefully

The key to working at home successfully is to minimise disturbance. Just as you wish to cause as little upset as possible to daily domestic operations, you also wish to be disturbed as little as possible. It is useful to set some ground rules and to agree them with those who share the household. Do give thought to:

- entertaining visitors – from both the business and family viewpoints
- noise levels
- heating, lighting, ventilation and security
- suitable workspace and equipment
- electrical and communications points.

5. Choose your office equipment equally carefully

Work out your needs, find out what is available and put together a realistic plan and budget. Do not buy expensive equipment for its own sake or because it is fashionable. 'What you need' should take priority over 'what would be nice'. Remember that computers are obsolescent in 4-5 years.

Consider first whether you will use a conveniently near secretarial and accounting service or whether you intend to do some, if not all, of the administrative work yourself. Assuming that you are going to do it yourself, you will need to consider:

- a computer
- a printer which meets your needs for quality
- a photocopier (but again you might use one available through an agency or as a publicly accessible facility)
- a modem
- suitable software
- a desk (second-hand?) and chair
- filing and storage facilities.

Weigh up the pros and cons of leasing versus purchasing and think of maintenance contracts which will keep you operational when (rather than if!) your equipment breaks down.

6. Select communications equipment which matches your needs

- Do you need an answerphone facility or a mobile telephone?
- Which telecommunications company offers the best deal for your business?
- How many telecommunications lines do you need?

- What about facilities such as call diversion and voice messaging?
- Is ISDN worth considering?
- Should you obtain a fax machine which can be used as a photocopier, printer, and answerphone?
- Do you need Internet facilities? Which access provider should you choose for email or for marketing on the World Wide Web?

7. Pay attention to security

- Ensure that you have your equipment well insured. Your domestic policy may not cover business equipment, so speak to your insurance company.
- Set up computer back-up systems, including copies of important data, as a precaution against fire, power failures, operator mistakes or burglary.
- Think hard before you advertise the presence of your business. If customers do not normally visit you, you don't need to display notices. Thieves will see them and consider your premises a 'prime target'! If you do display a notice, be sure that you do not first need the permission of your local authority.
- Install recommended security devices and burglar alarms. Your local Police Crime Prevention Officer will advise you.
- Ask your neighbours to keep an eye on your property when you are away and offer to do the same for them.
- Don't leave an 'I am away on holiday' message on your answerphone – it will invite burglars and it will suggest your business is not well established.
- Consider diverting your calls to a 'bureau' or colleague who is prepared to handle enquiries during your absence – callers expect you to get back to them within 24 hours.
- Make arrangements for your postman/couriers to leave packages with a neighbour when you are away.

8. Be mindful of neighbours' rights

- Don't rely on neighbours just to accept any disturbance your business may cause them. Talk to them before you start and establish mutual understanding.
- Ensure that legal provisions and requirements are clearly understood by all concerned. An injunction can be taken out against you operating your business if legalities or byelaws are breached. If nobody has complained for a long period of time, it may be held that what you are doing has become accepted. In this case the law will assume 'common practice'. You may apply to have restrictions removed – speak to your lawyer.

9. Consider 'buying in' supplies and services

'Buying in' will afford you flexibility and avoid the extra overheads that do-it-yourself will bring. It will also enable you to choose what you want, when you want it, at a known price, and help to establish and expand your business network.

- Establish exactly what service you require, obtain estimates for it and compare them with the cost (and time) of doing the work yourself.
- Decide which supplier you will use, bearing in mind your knowledge of the quality of goods and services, and the punctuality or courtesy they have provided to you or business colleagues in the past. If you have no foreknowledge, ask for the names of other customers whom you may approach.
- Agree clear terms for the business – quantities, delivery dates, prices, discounts – with the chosen supplier, confirming them in writing with your official order.
- Check any goods purchased on arrival and notify the supplier of any damage or discrepancies without delay. Thank your supplier and pay promptly. Establish a reputation as a prompt payer who expects prompt payment.

10. Establish a professional image for your home-based business

- Have well-designed stationery printed.
- Establish clear 'work/domestic' boundaries to maintain a 'professional' image for your business – callers will judge you by what they see and hear when they are visiting or telephoning you.
- Encourage your family to answer the telephone in a polite and helpful way. Prepare a short script for everyone to use, and ensure that there is a notepad and pencil by the telephone.
- Conduct any meetings at home as you would in an office and ensure you will not be disturbed.
- Consider the value of arranging meetings away from home if a large number of people will be attending – hotels or local business centres may be a better option.

11. Know yourself and manage yourself

- As far as possible establish a regular routine and set yourself clear tasks for each day.
- Use your diary to plan your activities.
- Remember to leave time for administration, or 'paperwork' will pile up.
- Don't underestimate the time required for 'clerical' activities – producing letters, arranging travel, etc. It can easily take up to 2–3 hours a day.
- Recognise when you are at your best. Is it morning, afternoon or evening? Plan to do your most demanding work at the most appropriate time of the day.
- Reward yourself for work well-done – a short walk, a cup of coffee or a relaxed look at the newspaper.

Useful reading

The new guide to working from home, Rev ed, Sue Read, London: Headline, 1995
Your home office, 2nd ed, Peter Chatterton, London: Kogan Page, 1995
Running a home based business, Diane M Baker, London: Kogan Page, 1994

Thought starters

- Don't expect your family to follow the rules if you don't.
- Do avoid the temptation of 'doing it in ten minutes' time' when you have a problem.
- Don't forget your customers.

Setting up as a Consultant

This checklist provides initial guidance for those thinking of setting up as a sole-trader management consultant. It concentrates solely on aspects of consultancy; more general advice on setting up a small business is covered by other checklists in this book.

MCI Standards

This checklist has relevance for the MCI Management Standards: Key Roles A and C – Manage Activities and Manage People.

Definition

A consultant provides, to clients, professional advice or services that the clients do not wish, for whatever reason, to provide for themselves.

Advantages of setting up as a consultant

By setting up as a consultant, you have:

- the ability to work on areas and issues of real interest to you
- the flexibility (within limits) to determine when and where you work
- the challenge and excitement of running your own business
- independence from other people – not having to work for someone else (apart from your clients!).

Disadvantages of becoming a consultant

You could face:

- loneliness and isolation if you set up on your own
- the lack of a regular income and other company benefits
- difficulties in separating work and home life
- a lack of job security.

Action checklist

1. Determine your area of specialisation

What kind of consultancy services will you offer? Describing yourself as a 'management' consultant is too broad if you are setting up alone. Try to determine what your market is now, what you want it to be in the future, and how you will get there. Examine your strengths and weaknesses [SWOT analysis]; choose one or two areas of specialisation based on your experience. Work out what it is that should attract clients to you as opposed to another consultant.

2. Carry out market research to decide your unique selling point(s)

Find out what opportunities there are within your chosen specialisations. These could relate to filling a gap in regional or market coverage, or providing a better or more personal service at lower cost. You will need to be able to make an assessment of:

- how much of a market there is for your specialisation and how much it is already being satisfied
- the competition, by researching their products and services and, more importantly, customers' views of them
- threats to existing markets and opportunities for new markets.

If the market looks to be small or overcrowded, go back again and consider in what other directions your knowledge or experience might be used. Be wary of trying to compete on price alone or of setting up at all if you cannot identify something you can provide that is not already being offered cost-effectively. If necessary, go through the market research process again.

3. Work out a charging strategy

Research market rates in your specialist area and the relevant geographical market – one source might be the Management Consultancy Information Service's Management Consultancy Fee Rate Survey (see Useful addresses). Offer a discount on the market rates to:

- compensate clients for the risk in employing you rather than an established firm
- reflect your lower overheads.

Do not charge too low a rate, however, as it is difficult to raise rates later if you discount too heavily at first. Remember too that clients like to feel they are receiving advice that is good value rather than cheap: clients are suspicious of cut-price consultancy

Calculate a realistic number of fee earning days. Exclude time for holidays (including public holidays), sickness and time spent marketing your services, attending courses, etc. Calculate your fees on the basis of 180-200 working days per year.

4. Plan your marketing strategy

- List your particular selling points. Put yourself in the position of a client trying to decide whether to employ you or an established consultant.
- Register with consultancy directories and agencies.
- Join a professional organisation, a network or other professional group of consultants.
- Write papers for publication or presentation at a conference.
- Give talks to appropriate local groups.
- Get in touch with recent contacts.

5. Secure your first client

Before you do anything else, find your first client. If you do not have a contract or potential contract from a former employer, trawl every existing business contact. Securing the first client will:

- make it easier for you to market to prospective new clients
- firm up your ideas about the type of business you want to become
- provide income.

6. Write the proposal

A winning proposal needs to show:

- knowledge of and experience in the area in question
- understanding of the client's requirements
- creativity and innovation in approaching the project.

The steps to ensure a comprehensive approach include:

- beginning by showing evidence of the three factors above
- carrying out research – with key people as well as consulting relevant library information
- showing creativity – in laying out ideas and possible solutions
- detailing your Unique Selling Point – what sets you apart from the rest
- addressing the competition – not by emphasising their weaknesses, but by focusing on your strengths
- clarifying your strategy – where you will take the client and how you will get them there
- determining costs and proposing budgets
- organising the proposal so that it is a document with some bite to it
- writing a summary and putting it at the beginning
- writing objectively, clearly and simply.

Check your draft proposal with a friend or colleague if possible.

7. Negotiate the contract

The contract is the vital stage which secures your client and determines the nature of the work to be done. It will also specify how you will be paid – by performance, percentage or daily rate – and what kind of expenses will be permissible. Coming out with the contract you want is down to your negotiation skills; there are always some areas for adjustment, just as there may well be some which are non-negotiable. It is important to be able to 'read' these in advance. Don't appear greedy, but don't be a soft touch either.

8. Conduct the assignment

Key steps to success include:

- keeping to budget and time
- understanding the client's organisational culture and language
- ensuring relevant staff are involved and consulted
- holding regular feedback sessions with your client
- maintaining a professional approach.

Dos and don'ts for setting up as a consultant

Do
- Minimise your start-up costs and keep a very tight control on outgoings for at least three months.
- Put everything possible into your first contract: maintaining excellent contacts with that client is the easiest way of securing new business.

Don't
- Be tempted to set up a business or incur any costs until you have secured your first client.
- Underestimate the costs of setting up or the delays in receiving payments from clients.

Useful reading

BOOKS

Management consulting: a guide to the profession, 3rd ed, Milan Kubr, Geneva: International Labour Office, 1996

The perfect consultant: all you need to get it right first time, Max Eggert and Elaine van der Zeil, London: Arrow Business Books, 1995

The business plan guide for independent consultants, Herman Holtz, New York: John Wiley, 1994

Starting a high income consultancy, James Essinger, London: Pitman, 1994

High income consulting: how to build and market your professional practice, Tom Lambert, London: Nicholas Brealey, 1993

JOURNAL ARTICLES

Alone against the world, David A Palmer, Training and Development UK, Vol 12 no 3, March 1994, pp24, 26, 28

Thinking of becoming an independent consultant?, Ian Jacobsen, Journal of Management Consulting, Vol 6 no 3, 1990, pp22–25

Useful addresses

Institute of Management Consultants, 5th Floor, 30-33 Hatton Gardens, London EC1N 8DL, Tel: 0171 242 2140

Management Consultancies Association, 11 West Halkin Street, London SW1X 8JL, Tel: 0171 235 3897

Management Consultancy Information Service, 38 Blenheim Avenue, Gants Hill, Ilford, Essex IG2 6JQ, Tel: 0181 554 4695

Thought starters

- What plans do you have to maintain and develop your expertise?
- What advantage can you offer over the competition?
- Think about networking with, as opposed to competing against, the competition.

Writing a Business Plan

This checklist is designed as an aid to those responsible for construct-
ing a business plan and provides a sequential framework for its
compilation. The success of the business plan will depend as much on
the clarity and realism of the thought behind it as on how it is
expressed and put together.

MCI standards

This checklist has relevance for the MCI Management Standards: Key Roles
A and B – Manage Activities and Manage Resources.

Definition

A business plan is not only a requisite for seeking finance from investors,
but also an essential document to describe aims and objectives and enable
measurement of progress towards achieving them. The business plan provides the means to:

- appraise the present and future of the business
- work out short- and long-term objectives
- establish a framework for action to achieve those objectives.

It consists, essentially, of three elements: the operations plan, the financial
plan and the marketing plan.

- The **operations plan** will include supply of raw materials, technological
  requirements, key processes, resource needs and production and delivery
  targets.
- The **financial plan** will assess fixed and variable costs and dictate mini-
  mum financial requirements.
- The **marketing plan** will cover how market intelligence will be gathered
  and ensure that the organisation's strategies will meet market needs.

Advantages

Clear business plans:

- form a yardstick by which to measure performance
- are the starting-point for departmental or divisional operational plans
- provide a framework for offering incentives to managers

- demonstrate that the organisation knows where it is going
- form the bridge between the organisation's strategy and what people should actually do
- can assist in attracting major customers, financial assistance and shareholders' support.

Disadvantages

They require:

- detailed thought, research and application
- the clearest expression to stand up against incomprehension and criticism
- honest and realistic appraisal of organisational shortcomings, problems and obstacles, as well as the rosy side
- writing from the reader's point of view, not the writer's
- regular monitoring and modification if appropriate
- acceptance by, not just imposition on, all the key players in the organisation.

Action checklist

Before you start it is often valuable to carry out a SWOT – Strengths, Weaknesses, Opportunities, Threats – analysis of your organisation, or the sector concerned; it will help to provide a keener focus for working out objectives and for drafting the plan. Remember too that the SWOT does not just involve consideration of the past and present; it can include the future especially in terms of markets, customers and technology.

As a general rule the plan should be not more than about 25-30 pages with strongest focus on the management and financial elements. The executive summary should be no more than two pages.

1. Set the context

Describe:

- the background of the business, product or service
- who the customers are and when the business started
- brief summary of past performance
- any key or influential elements which might dictate the success of the product or service.

2. Define the objectives

Develop a list of short-term, specific targets that will help to indicate progress towards longer-term ones. Measurability is important.

3. Perform a market analysis

Persuade the reader/investor that the product/service will secure a substantial market. Include:

- a brief description of the overall market, and the specific market segment targeted
- detailed information on current and proposed customers
- names of leading competitors, market share, alternative products or services
- market influences – economic trends, seasonal fluctuations, legislation, social factors.

Are you aware of who and where your target market is and of what changes are affecting that market?

4. Propose your approach to marketing (the marketing plan)

Describe the marketing strategy used to approach customers by detailing:

- the image of the organisation you wish to convey
- a description of the promotional and publicity material
- the key or unique features which will differentiate the product
- the 4 Ps of marketing
- channels of distribution.

What marketing methods do your competitors use and how effective are they?

5. Describe your plans for development and production (the operations plan)

Focus on all aspects of researching, developing, producing and delivering your product or service. Describe the research, development and production processes with expected costs of raw materials, labour, plant and equipment. Include a brief section on contingency planning for the prospect that things may go wrong.

Are you aware of the terms and conditions of your main suppliers? Are you aware of the steps you need to take to maintain quality?

6. Clarify the current financial situation (the financial plan)

Lay out exactly what is required of the investors. The financial plan is composed principally of figures of past, present and projected performance including any start-up costs, profit-loss statements, cash flow analyses and balance sheet data. Repayment will be of key interest to the investor so include accurate break-even projections. It is also important to demonstrate how sound financial control will be exercised over borrowed and incoming funds. Make sure you can support your sales forecast with reasons for your assumptions and opt for caution rather than for the rosiest scenario.

Can the business realistically support the level of borrowing needed to get it launched?

7. Demonstrate how management is both committed and capable

Describe your strengths and skills. An organisation chart should mark out capabilities as well as responsibilities. If there are weaknesses, propose how they will be dealt with.

8. Describe the ownership of the organisation

An investor will need to know the legal constitution of the organisation – partnership, limited liability, corporation. Show how much investment is already being made and by whom.

9. Include risks and problems and critical success factors

Do not omit the negative factors, both actual and potential. Demonstrate that you are aware of likely changes in, for example, information technology, markets or economic circumstances. Show that you will be ready to correct over-spending or failure to meet deadlines.

Provide a brief account of the critical success factors such as:

- the learning environment which generates success
- specialists and technicians with their knowledge and networks
- how the team can respond to adversity and turn things round.

10. Conclude with the impression you want to leave

The conclusion summarises the key features such as, strategic direction, strengths and unique benefits, projected (realistic) sales and returns. Include a proposed time-table of events to strengthen the image of sound planning. The conclusion sets the scene for the executive summary.

11. Provide an executive summary

Written last, but appears first. Include the unique features of the product(s) or service(s); the current, mid- and long-term direction of the organisation; the product/service benefits to the defined market sector; the qualities and skills of the people who will make it all happen; a financial statement of assets, sales/profits expectations and how much capital is required; and, as a conclusion, a statement of return for the investor.

Dos and don'ts for writing a business plan

Do

- Keep it short, focused and readable.
- Research the target readership.
- Draft and re-draft to improve it.
- Organise it effectively.
- Consult as widely as appropriate.
- Address fully any possible bones of contention.
- Outline the qualities and skills of the management team.
- Use diagrams and charts for clarity.
- Use the simplest language possible to avoid possible misunderstandings.
- Provide an executive summary.

Don't

- Be too optimistic in estimating income potential or enthusiastic reaction.
- Neglect to point out the 'obvious' benefits of the product or service.
- Use long words, technical jargon and long sentences.
- Make assumptions on the reader's behalf.
- Neglect help from appropriate sources such as accountants or banks.
- Forget who you are writing for.
- Forget the contingency aspects of the plan.

Useful reading

BOOKS

Preparing a business plan: how to lay the right foundations for business success, 2nd ed, Matthew Record, Plymouth: How to Books, 1997

Successful business plans in a week, 2nd ed, Iain Maitland, London: Hodder & Stoughton, 1998

JOURNAL ARTICLES

How to write a great business plan, William A Sahlman, Harvard Business Review, vol 75 no 4, Jul/Aug 1997, pp98–108

How to write a winning business plan, W Keith Schilit, Business Horizons, Sept–Oct 1987, pp13–22

Thought starters

- What is your main business?
- Who are your main customers?
- What is your main capability?
- How healthy – really – is the current financial situation?
- Whom are you trying to convince?

Five Routes to Greater Profitability

This checklist identifies five routes which are frequently taken in pursuit of greater profitability. Many businessmen and managers are familiar with them under a variety of labels, but too many fail to recognise the interrelationships between them. A change in any one of them has a potential impact on the others – a fact often ignored, to the detriment of the business.

MCI Standards

This checklist has relevance for the MCI Management Standards: Key Role B – Manage Resources.

Definition

There are five basic ways in which a firm can have a direct effect on its profitability. These are:

- increasing sales volume
- reducing costs and/or ensuring that costs are fully recovered where this has not previously been the case
- improving product-mix (varying the relationships between the volumes of individual products or groups of products sold)
- raising prices selectively or as a whole
- reducing the capital employed in the business.

A change in any one of these will impact on the others. Any change, made or planned, whether voluntary or involuntary, must therefore be considered in the context of all the others; changes made in isolation may not have the expected impact on profitability. Other management strategies, such as total quality management and customer service programmes, can also influence profitability by cutting out unneeded processes for example, or motivating staff to greater output.

Advantages of recognising the interrelationships of the five strategic factors

- Financial planning will take all five factors and their interrelationships into account.
- The impact on profitability of changes can be assessed systematically.
- The risks associated with changes can be viewed more realistically.
- The line between risk taking and recklessness may be clearer.

Action checklist

1. Consider increasing your sales volume

Increasing sales volume may appear to be an easy way of increasing the profitability of your organisation, but this is not necessarily the case. There are certain points that must be recognised.

- Selling more and more is not the key to increased profitability: profit requires turnover, but turnover does not equal profit. Remember that 'turnover is vanity: profit is sanity'.
- If you increase your sales volume, you must simultaneously rigorously control costs, prices, capital employed and your product/service mix. Be sure that none of the latter components of your potential profitability increase disproportionately. If they do, increased sales will lead to reduced rather than increased profit.
- Seeking to increase your sales turnover by employing an additional representative or trading in a bigger geographical area will only produce more profit if extra sales produce at least enough extra profit (not revenue) to cover the extra costs.
- If prices and margins are reduced to generate more sales, a considerable increase in sales will be necessary, otherwise total revenue will fall while costs remain the same.
- Increases in small volume orders may hinder profitability rather than boost it due to the inherent order administration costs, such as invoicing and dispatching.
- If credit is extended in order to encourage more sales your organisation will have to bear the costs of this – with a knock-on effect on profitability.
- Selling more of all your product/service lines and/or introducing new ones may increase your sales volume, but be sure you know the contribution that each product/service line makes. Selling more of loss-making lines is bad business unless it is necessary in order to raise sales of profit-making ones.
- In some circumstances greater profits may be achieved if turnover is reduced. Surveys have shown that a wholly disproportionate amount of

cost and effort can be invested to achieve a small amount of turnover and sales revenue. It is not uncommon to find that 50% of deliveries made account for only 15% of sales revenue. Consider what would happen if you reduced your sales by a selective 10%.

2. Look at the possibility of reducing your costs

Investigate and establish your true costs in total and for unit sales. You cannot adjust your costs in relation to other parts of your business unless you know what they are. Consider the effects of specific cost reductions carefully – arbitrary reductions may not produce the desired results in the long term. Seek advice from your accountant (internal), your auditors, and your bank manager.

3. Analyse and improve your product/service mix

Product/service mix reflects the combinations in which the products/services you provide are sold. The mix is normally derived from a series of historical accidents rather than from careful planning and analysis and consequently may not be the most profitable for your organisation.

Examine the products sold by your organisation in terms of the costs attributable to each and the net margin each makes. You may find that those products which produce the highest unit gross profit and which make the highest percentage contribution to your volume of sales also attract a disproportionate amount of your selling costs.

You may find, for example, that you should aim to sell more of A and B which you have found to be profitable, to supply less of C and D which are of limited profitability and to eliminate E and F from your sales portfolio as they are loss makers. Consider the impact this will have on other factors – for example a well-founded change in the product/service mix may lead to a reduced volume of sales but increased profitability.

4. Examine your selling prices and profit margins

Raising selling prices is a potential route to increased profitability (or at least to maintaining current levels of profitability when they may otherwise fall), but there are of course pitfalls. Although price increases may be accepted if they are part of a general adjustment of prices in your business sector (in which case your overall level of profitability is likely to be merely maintained), to raise prices in isolation without losing business (and thereby risking reduced profits) requires either a near monopoly situation, a vast difference between your products and those of your competitors, or a carefully thought-out (and enacted) policy and sales strategy.

5. Look at the capital employed in your business

Obtaining good returns on capital and reducing the capital tied up in your business normally lead to improved profitability.

Identify the categories of capital employed in your business and consider whether the following can apply to these categories:

- introducing tighter control of credit
- reducing stock levels
- introducing outsourcing (or expanding its scope)
- disposing of redundant buildings (or even locating to a new site where better terms of lease may be available).

Make sure you take professional advice.

6. Remember balance

A healthy business in a competitive environment is always changing, and as demonstrated here, this is particularly relevant to the five components of profitability and their interrelationships. Change, particularly in the area of aiming to improve profitability, always requires compromise, and your aim must be to achieve the best balance possible between sales volume, costs, margins, product-mix and capital employed – the ideal balance is often impossible, and this year's optimum may not be next year's.

Dos and don'ts for increasing profitability

Do
- Identify which of the five categories any proposed change falls into.
- Carefully consider the impact of change on all categories.
- Consider longer term impacts on the capacity of business to survive as well as on its profitability.

Don't
- Ignore the 'bad news' which may emerge from analysis when it threatens the achievement of a pet ambition, such as expansion into other lines or into another country.
- Ignore changes which may be imposed on your business, by the bank manager or legislation for example.

Useful reading
Books
Survival tactics: how to make profits in difficult times, John Yates, London: Mercury Books, 1992
Improve your profits, Malcolm Bird, London: Piatkus, 1991

How to control your costs and increase your profits: over 400 practical cost control ideas, David M Martin, Hemel Hempstead: Director Books in association with the Institute of Directors, 1992

JOURNAL ARTICLE

Improving profitability through product tirage, Robert G Docters, Business Horizons, Jan/Feb, vol 39 no 1, 1996, pp71–78

Thought starters

- Have you sometimes ignored the interrelationships in the past? What happened?
- The first priority in any business must be survival. Do proposed changes threaten the survival of your business?
- Is a proposed change based on necessity, opportunity or vanity?

Franchising your Business

This checklist provides guidance to those who wish to expand their business through the sale of franchises.

Franchising is a technique for business expansion, both for the small one-location company and the national multi-outlet organisation. It is often said to be one of the safest means of achieving growth, and although it does have many advantages, it still requires careful planning to be successful.

Examples of large organisations that use franchising to expand include McDonalds, Tie Rack, and Swinton Insurance. A large number and variety of small businesses have used franchising, including Dial-A-Duster, Mobile Phone Centre, and Magic Windshields UK.

MCI Standards

This checklist has relevance for the MCI Management Standards: Key Roles A and B – Manage Activities and Manage Resources.

Definition

For the purposes of this checklist the term franchising refers to a 'Business Concept Franchise'. This involves: the franchisor, who lends his trademark or trade name and his business system to the franchisee, who pays a royalty and often an initial fee for the right to do business under the franchisor's name and system.

Advantages of franchising your business

Franchising:

- provides an affordable means of accelerating expansion
- spreads the financial risk of expansion
- means that products or goods can be bought in bulk to cover the whole franchise network, thus increasing profit margins and competitiveness.

Disadvantages of franchising your business

Franchising does have some drawbacks, in that:

- some control and profit are lost by engaging a third party
- conflicts can arise between the franchisor and the franchisee
- returns are low until the franchise network has been built up.

Action checklist

1. Take stock

Define what has made your business a success so far and then ask yourself:

- is it a unique or new concept that has the potential to expand locally, nationally or even internationally?
- are the operating systems of the concept polished, efficient and replicable?
- would it be relatively easy to train others in the use of the systems and procedures?
- are the profit margins built into the concept large enough so that every franchisee could realise an attractive return on their investment?
- is the franchise affordable enough to attract a number of franchisees?

If you've answered yes to the above questions then there is a good chance that you can franchise your business.

2. Obtain legal advice

As what you are 'selling' is really your trademark (or trade name), make sure that it is legally yours and that any one found copying it can be prosecuted. Your name or trademark must be registered at the Trade Marks Registry (see Useful addresses).

3. Draw up a business plan

The business plan provides the means to:

- appraise the present and future of the business
- work out short- and long-term objectives
- establish a framework for action to achieve those objectives.

Your bank should be able to help you do this if you need assistance. This will help you to identify how quickly you can expand, who your competitors are, and whether or not your system will be able to compete with them.

4. Define the franchise package

Work out exactly what you will be offering the franchisee, including:

- the concept – trademark and/or trade name
- initial assistance – finding premises for example
- continuing training and advice
- bulk purchasing power
- sharing the cost of national advertising.

You can also include other areas, such as help with accounts and IT equipment.

The package should also lay out what each franchisee will have to pay. You may choose a royalty only payment (leave plenty of room for the franchisee to make a profit). You may also wish to charge an initial and annual fee but if these are set too high it may discourage applicants.

5. Draw up a contract

Take professional legal advice over the franchise contract to make it watertight. If the selected franchisee does not perform to the required standard you should ensure that you can regain control of the franchise.

6. Prepare a pilot

It is very important that you test out your franchise concept in one particular area. By doing this you will find out the best ways of recruiting and selecting franchisees, and the kind of support they need to start up. The lessons learned from the pilot will prove invaluable to the success of your franchising network.

7. Advertise the franchise

Place adverts in the local newspapers of your pilot area, and in national franchise journals such as Franchise Magazine or Franchise World (see Useful addresses). Highlight the attractions of running a franchise of your concept, including your success so far and the market need. You will need a brochure to help 'sell' the franchise. Obtain outside help if you do not have the resources necessary in-house to produce a professional-looking document.

8. Select a franchisee

Selecting the right franchisee is vital, as no matter how sound your business concept and trade name, the franchisee will be the person responsible for 'sales' in their area. Increasing the number of franchises will be much easier if you can prove that the concept has been successful.

Look into the backgrounds of the applicants carefully. Are they enthusiastic and hard-working, or are they likely to give up at the first sign of difficulty? You will never be 100% certain that an applicant has got what it takes, but your business instinct will give you a good idea.

9. Start the pilot

Provide as much support as possible to get this first franchise off the ground. Give advice when it is needed, but be prepared to let the franchisee use their own initiative and don't 'crowd' them. Remember that now you have sold the franchise it is as much the franchisee's business as it is yours.

10. Monitor the franchise

Learn from the results of the franchise pilot. It may mean that you have to revise elements of the franchise package such as royalty paid or training given. Get the franchisee's opinion by asking if there were any problems with the franchise and what other help would have been useful.

11. Advertise again

You may wish to run further pilots, or, if the initial one was a success, you may wish to expand as quickly as you can get franchisees. However, remember that you will need to provide help, advice and training as well as all the resourcing for your franchise network.

12. Review the franchise on a regular basis

You should never allow your franchise to become static. Make changes to the concept and the package you offer as necessary. Review each franchisee annually and decide whether you will renew their contract, look for another franchisee, or regain control yourself.

Dos and don'ts when franchising your business

Do
- Get legal advice about securing your trade name or trademark and when drawing up a contract with the franchisee.
- Select regions for franchising and suitable franchisees with care.
- Remember how long it took for you to get a foothold in the market – be patient with the franchisee.
- Make sure that you can regain control of the franchise if necessary at the end of the franchise agreement.

Don't

- Forget to pilot the franchise first.
- Just leave the franchisee to it without providing advice and training.
- Be too restrictive in the franchise contract – allow for innovation by the franchisee.

Useful reading

BOOK

The United Kingdom franchise directory, Norwich: Franchise Development Services

JOURNAL ARTICLES

Assessing the franchise option, Surinder Tikoo, Business Horizons, vol 39 no 3, May / Jun 1996, pp78–82

Franchising your business, Small Business Confidential, no 89, Jan 1991, pp8–10

Useful addresses

British Franchise Association, Thames View, Newtown Road, Henley-on-Thames, Oxon, RG9 1HG, Tel: 01491 578 049

Franchise Development Services Ltd, Castle House, Castle Meadow, Norwich, NR2 1PJ, Tel: 01603 630174, Publishers of Franchise Magazine

Franchise World, James House, 37 Nottingham Road, London, SW17 7EA, Tel: 0181 767 1371

The Trade Marks Registry, 25 Southampton Buildings, London, WC2A 1AW, Tel: 0171 438 4700

Each of the major high street banks has its own franchising department which can offer advice.

Thought starters

- What have been the secrets of your business success?
- What advice would have helped you when you first started your business?
- What were the most difficult periods when building up your business?

Drawing up a Budget

This checklist is for managers who have responsibility for drawing up and presenting a budget.

Budgeting is at the heart of the way organisations measure what they want to achieve. It is a key planning device and one that organisations are increasingly democratising. Drawing up a budget is no longer the sole province of accountants and finance directors. These days everyone in the organisation has a role to play in drawing up a budget. There is no room for financially naive managers in today's organisations.

Drawing up a budget involves a mix of number skills and people skills like negotiation and listening – it is not a mechanistic process. It is dynamic and involves managers throughout the organisation.

MCI Standards

This checklist has relevance for the MCI Management Standards: Key Roles B and G – Manage Resources and Manage Projects.

Definition

A budget is a statement of expenditure or income that has been allocated under a set of headings, for a set period of time.

Advantages of budgeting

Budgets:
- are a key tool in the achievement of a company's strategic plan
- help managers in different parts of the organisation to coordinate their activities
- are a way of helping managers take financial responsibility
- are an effective way of allocating funds and planning
- are a way of communicating important financial information
- are motivating – they set clear goals
- help managers to think about the future and set plans
- help managers to measure their own performance and the performance of their team.

Disadvantages of failing to budget (or budgeting poorly)

Poor budgeting or no budgeting at all presents a whole range of disadvantages including:

- unreliable financial information
- a breakdown in financial control.

Action checklist

1. Identify the key plans and objectives for the organisation

You need to identify these objectives so that you know what over-riding factors to consider when preparing your budget. Budgeting is to some extent a secondary process – secondary to the strategic or business plans of the organisation. Only when these are clear can a suitable budget be prepared.

Is it, for example, a budget for growth or for standing still? This will affect the way you draw up figures.

2. Determine the key or limiting factors

Every organisation has some factors which limit its growth. In most cases this is the volume of sales, or the number of customers, or the amount of manufacturing plant available. Whatever they are, these key factors have significance for planning and budgeting. There's no point drawing up a superb budget based on selling a high volume if either it is unrealistic to reach this level of sales or your organisation couldn't handle the work load to reach the figure.

3. What is coming in?

Look at the range of sources – are you generating funds, or is money allocated at the beginning of each year? Will you really get in all the money you have noted down, or will some come in the next financial year, or fall through? How much of it is guaranteed income?

4. What is going out?

Estimate your expected costs. Break down costs under different headings. The range of cost headings usually include those related to:

- staffing, wages, pensions, training etc
- premises, rent, repairs, heating etc
- a company's legal duties
- materials used – stationery, telephone, raw materials
- any other business costs, such as insurance, company tax etc.

The general principle is to divide the budget up under whatever headings seem sensible to you – but, as organisations often group headings together, ensure there is a degree of commonality across the company. Look at last year's budget and use the headings in it as a starting point.

5. Think through the fixed and variable costs

There are two types of costs:

- **fixed costs** – those costs you have no matter how much extra work the organisation handles, such as permanent staff costs
- **variable costs** – costs that are dependent on the organisation's level of work, such as how much raw material is bought or how much advertising is carried out.

Ask your finance section to help you identify your fixed and variable costs.

6. Decide how to draw up the budget

There are different theories about how you should begin to draw up a budget.

Incremental budgeting – this is based on using last year's figures. If you use this method you would base a budget on how last year's went – with, of course, an adjustment to take things like inflation into account. This is a quick and simple way of putting together a first draft of a budget but if last year's budget was wrong you keep adding to your mistakes. It is also a conservative approach, making the assumption that present objectives are right and that there is a high degree of continuity.

If you are using an incremental approach, work out how far last year's budget actually reflected reality. Write down:

- the budget
- the way it actually worked – what you actually spent
- the variance – how far was the budget out, and why?

Zero-based budgeting – here an analysis of each cost from fresh at the start of each year is made. Analyse each cost as the picture looks now rather than referring to the budget of the previous year. This is a fundamental approach, requiring you to justify every item and redefine your objectives.

7. Collect all the information you need to set this year's budget

Look at last year's budget and learn what you can for this year's. Make sure you have spoken to all the stakeholders before drawing up the budget to make sure they've had an input and you have not missed anything.

Look at the organisation's objectives and targets to see if and how your budget needs to be adjusted or reconstructed.

Assess all external and internal factors which may have a bearing on your performance. These may include: the rate of inflation, bank lending rates, trade prospects which are forecast for the following year, and whether you wish to stimulate the market (and therefore the resources, money, people and equipment necessary to do so). Budgeting for growth also means having the available resources to handle the increased levels of business if the marketing works, otherwise you will be stimulating a demand you cannot meet.

8. Ask some important questions

The following questions will help to prepare the budget accurately.

- Am I clear about strategic objectives and how they affect my area of responsibility?
- Have I accurately forecast the number of people the job requires to meet objectives?
- Are there likely to be any changes?
- Am I clear about the income?
- Am I clear about outgoings?
- Are there any factors on the horizon that might throw the forecast into chaos?

9. Draw up the budget

Keep detailed notes on why you have included the figures you have in your budget. It may seem obvious when you write it down, but you might not remember how you calculated your budget in six months' time. Remember to build in an allowance for contingency – the 'what if' – for things that may go wrong. This may reflect on the revenue targets foreseen if levels of business do not meet expectations, or on controlling expenditure early in the financial year until you obtain a clearer picture of how your budget is performing.

10. Build in budget control parameters

You or your finance department will need to track income and expenditure against the budget. This may be monthly, weekly or even daily, depending on the business. See the checklist on controlling budgets for more information.

11. Present the budget

If you have to make a presentation on the budget to senior managers or colleagues in addition to the written statement, then make sure you present a picture of reality, with possible down-turns and problems, rather than attempting to impress. If it looks optimistic, say so and why; if it looks pessimistic, make sure you convey the appropriate message.

Dos and don'ts for drawing up a budget

Do

- Be realistic.
- Take last year's budget and actual result (what you really spent) into account.
- Be aware of fixed and variable costs.
- Develop budget headings that work, both for you and for the organisation as a whole.
- Collect information thoroughly.
- Decide whether to go for a zero-based or incremental approach.

Don't

- Be over-optimistic.
- Leave too little time.
- Draw up a budget without involving others.

Useful reading

BOOKS

Finance and budgeting for line managers, Anthony Greenall, London: Industrial Society, 1996

Budgeting for non financial managers: how to master and maintain effective budgets, Iain Maitland, London: Pitman, 1996

Successful budgeting in a week, Malcolm Secrett, London: Hodder & Stoughton, 1993

JOURNAL ARTICLES

The link between budgeting, corporate planning and strategic management, Peter Trim, Journal of European Business Education, Vol 5 no 2, May 1996 pp26–35

Budgeting from pain to power, Robert G Finney, Management Review, Vol 82 no 9, September 1993, pp27–31

Thought starters

- Do you understand the major objectives laid down within your organisation's current strategic plan?
- Do you know how your area of responsibility fits within the current strategic plan?
- Have you listened carefully to all the stakeholders?
- Have you checked last year's budget?
- Have you drawn up a list of budget headings?
- Have you left enough time for the process?

Controlling a Budget

This checklist is for all managers who have budgetary responsibility. Budgetary control is at the heart of many managers' jobs. The skills of budgetary control are increasingly being valued in organisations. What is more, the ability to control a budget is now seen as an important factor in measuring performance and even as a passport to promotion.

Managers need to use a mix of skills when controlling budgets – gathering and using information; setting up early warning systems; taking decisions and monitoring results – all key management skills.

MCI Standards

This checklist has relevance for the MCI Management Standards: Key Role B – Manage Resources.

Definition

Budgetary control is achieved by comparing actual costs, revenues and performances against the set budget. It is necessary to carry out this comparison in order that the manager can, if they need to, take corrective action and make changes to their operational plans as required to keep them on budget.

Advantages of controlling budgets

- It is the only way in which you can monitor an organisation/team's financial performance.
- It allows managers to be clear about their department's financial position.
- It gives information on which to base action.

Disadvantages of failing to control a budget

If you fail to control your budget, you will:

- frequently over or underspend – not achieving what you planned
- lack up-to-date information which would explain why the actual results will be at variance with the budget
- demonstrate that your team/department/work is out of control – and that is a bad advertisement both for your company and for yourself.

Action checklist

1. Understand the figures

Make sure you understand how the figures in the budget are made up. You need to be clear about which figures you control and will be held responsible for and which are out of your control. For instance, if staff costs are higher because you sanctioned too much overtime you may be held responsible for that budget over-run, but if staff costs are higher because the union negotiated a higher than expected pay rise you **may** neither be held responsible for the over-run nor exercise control over it.

Only when you know which elements of the budget you are responsible for can you control it.

2. Speak to your accounts department

Find out what reports they can produce for you. This will save you extra work, give you accurate figures to work from and help you keep in touch with them – important, as they are a key stakeholder.

3. Set up a monitoring/early warning system

This will help you keep track of your costs and income. A paper system (keeping a tally of the costs incurred and checking them at the end of the month) works for small budgets, but both these and larger ones can benefit from the use of all available systems and information.

4. Decide on the appropriate time to monitor your budget

Choose a time which fits in with your organisation's and team's other commitments, perhaps:

● weekly
● monthly
● quarterly

and then stick to these review periods. It is important to get the time scale right – over-monitor and you waste time; under-monitor and you won't stay in control of things.

5. Identify variances

Use the information you've collected to identify variances from your original budget – both positive and negative. A negative variance means you have spent more than you planned – so you will need to look hard at the effect this will have on the year's performance and review your plans. A positive variance will mean you have underspent.

6. Don't assume a positive variance is a good thing

Analyse any variance – find out why it is happening and what effect it will have on the year's activity. Is it a one-off payment that has not been invoiced – a blip rather than a trend? Is it a surprising drop in interest rates, and will it continue? Are you not carrying out the marketing activities you planned? Have you failed to recruit a key member of staff?

7. Tell the right people

If you find you have a problem get information about it to the right people. For instance talk to:

● your boss
● your company accountant
● your team.

People often won't know there's a problem until you tell them. And until everyone who needs to know does know, you can't act. But remember that the communication process is two-way, and your team members may also be able to give early warnings of problems. Discuss the variances with your team and find out why they happened. They may have up-to-the-minute information on why things went wrong.

8. Now act

There is a range of different options, depending on the circumstances:

● do nothing if you anticipate the budget will come back into line, but make sure you can prove this, and review your monitoring period to ensure that what you expect happens
● prepare a forecast (or revise your forecast) on where you expect to be compared to your budget
● suggest corrective action to bring your budget back into line with the original budget. For instance, cut back on costs, try to increase sales, or put in a bid for underspends elsewhere.

Once you have decided what to do, make sure that all the right people know what your plans are, understand them and have time to comment if necessary. Then, be seen to act.

9. Keep monitoring the budget

Monitoring is an on-going process. Don't assume because you've put a problem right that there will never be another. Keep monitoring the budget and it will help you either to make sure it is back in line or hasn't got even further out of control.

10. Communicate any changes

If you have re-forecast, tell all the budget stakeholders – especially if they have to implement the change.

Dos and don'ts for controlling a budget

Do
- Communicate – upwards, downwards and across.
- Take action when you need to.
- Keep monitoring.

Don't
- Act rashly without thinking through the implications.
- Go it alone – always involve others.
- Hide the problem or ignore it – it won't go away.

Useful reading

BOOKS
Budgeting for non financial managers: how to master and maintain effective budgets, Iain Maitland, London: Pitman, 1996
Budgeting: profit planning and control, Glenn A Welsch, Ronald W Hilton, Paul N Gordon, 5th ed, Englewood Cliffs NJ: Prentice Hall International, 1988

JOURNAL ARTICLES
Budgeting from pain to power, Robert G Finney, Management Review, Vol 82 no 9, September 1993, pp27–31
ABC of budgeting and cash flow projections, Kim McMaster, Management NZ, Vol 33 no 7, October 1986, pp70–72

Thought starters

- Have you set up practical monitoring systems?
- Do your monitoring systems provide you with the information that you can act on to re-gain control?
- Have you collected all the information you can about why things have gone wrong?
- Have you communicated thoroughly?
- Have you planned your action carefully?

Cash Flow for the Small Business

This checklist is designed to help you develop understanding and control of cash flow in your business.

MCI Standards

This checklist has relevance for the MCI Management Standards: Key Role B – Manage Resources.

Definition

The flow of cash through a business may be likened to the flow of water through a central heating system. Too little cash/water or factors impeding a smooth and continuous flow of cash/water, create problems. Without an adequate flow of cash, a company may be trading profitably in the shorter term, but will nevertheless collapse. The figure on the next page illustrates the flow of cash through a business. The flow starts at (1) when the would-be owners of the business (or shareholder(s) if it is to be a limited company) invest funds, which go into the pool of cash (2).

This investment may not be a once and for all step. There may be subsequent investments for a variety of positive (such as business expansion) or negative (such as shortage of liquid funds) reasons. At the same time, or again later, lenders (3) may also put funds into the cash pool. The lenders may be the firm's bankers or, in some cases, members of the family or friends of the owners of the business.

To enable the firm to start trading we will assume that it obtains goods and services (4) on credit from suppliers (5) who become creditors. Consideration will be given to obtaining fixed assets. These may range from freehold buildings to office equipment, from lorries to cars. You will recognise that if acquisition is based on purchase, and if relevant assets are truly fixed, some liquid capital has been immobilised immediately. Cash also flows out of the 'pool' in the form of salaries and wages (7) and other expenses (8), which may include, for example, stationery and additional computer software.

If the new firm is to manufacture, it will require raw materials (9) – another outflow of cash, sooner if the materials are paid for immediately, 'not so much later' if they are purchased on credit. The expenditure of wages and other expenses (for example tools), together with the use of some of the raw materials (7), (8) and (9), will lead to the creation of saleable stocks (10). If the firm does not manufacture products for sale, it will purchase saleable stocks for resale. The stocks will join 'the stream' on their sale and will probably be sold on credit to customers who become debtors (11). They will owe the firm the price of goods or services supplied until they pay. When they do pay, cash will continue to flow back into the cash pool (2).

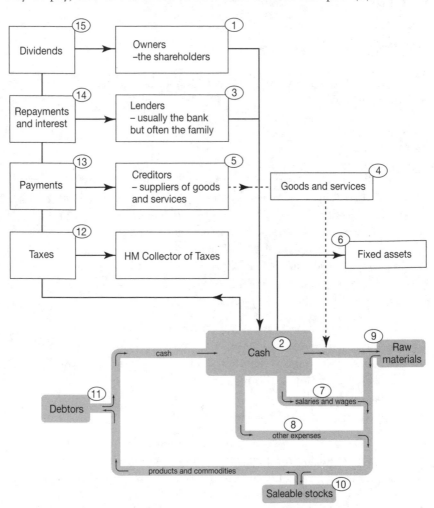

Sadly, the cycle is not complete. At the appropriate time, cash will be moved from the pool to pay taxes (12), to make payments to creditors (13), to make repayments of capital and payments of interest to lenders (14) and to make payments of dividends or other forms of reward to the owners, the original investors (15). It may be worthwhile to start again at (1) and to fol-low the sequence of the flow of cash through to (15). The sequence is never ending. If it stops, there is an explosion and, as in the case of central heating, the whole system will stop. Without an injection of cash, trading will cease and the firm will be wound up.

Advantages of controlling cash flow

- You know where your cash flow is tied up.
- You can spot potential bottlenecks and act to reduce their impact.
- You reduce your dependence on your bankers and save interest charges.
- You are in control of your business and can make informed decisions.

Action checklist

1. Identify the potential cash bottlenecks through your firm

A careful examination of the figure on the previous page may suggest bottlenecks at:

- fixed assets (6)
- raw materials (9)
- saleable stocks (10)
- debtors (11).

Examine these bottlenecks in turn.

2. Reconsider your investment in fixed assets

- Is cash unnecessarily tied up in fixed assets?
- Is it tied up in assets which are not used or could be disposed of?
- Is it tied up in necessary assets which could be replaced by leasing?
- Is it tied up in assets which represent a greater than necessary investment which could be replaced by something more modest?
- Has cash been invested in fixed assets for reasons of prestige rather than of profit?

3. Reconsider your investment in raw materials

- Have you tied up cash in raw materials to take advantage of special terms offered by suppliers?
- Are you sure that the advantages outweigh the costs of holding stocks which may not be used immediately? Against the advantages must be weighed:
  - the cost of borrowing money to finance stockholding
  - the loss of alternative uses for the capital employed
  - the costs of physical storage
  - the risks of stock shrinkage.

Likewise reconsider your investment in saleable stocks.

4. Reconsider an appropriate system of stock control

An appropriate system of stock control does not necessarily presuppose precise stock records for every line held in stock. The type of records adopted will depend on common sense. The cost of the system must be weighed against a financial evaluation of the problems which the system is intended to help solve.

Some form of control is necessary to guard against theft, obsolescence, spoilage, running out or having too much or an unbalanced stock, any of which can penalise a business severely. The basic requirements of a stock control system may be summarised as:

- a forecast of what you expect to sell and when
- a knowledge of your present stocks, updated at regular intervals
- a record of supplies received and deliveries made which should be periodically reconciled with present stocks (this reconciliation need not be of everything but only of selected items in sequence)
- predetermined and regularly reviewed re-order levels and quantities
- a knowledge of price trends, quantity discounts and the time which will elapse from the placing of an order until delivery.

Check stock at least once a year. Have you considered a perpetual inventory system or a cyclical stocktaking procedure using staff as and when fluctuating work loads make this possible? Are your stocks neatly stored in a way that makes stocktaking easy and eliminates the risk of contamination, obsolescence and damage?

5. Look carefully at your systems for granting and controlling credit

There is a direct relationship between the amount and length of credit allowed and the return on capital and net profit which a firm can make. It is assumed that in most cases it is more important to obtain the quickest possible turnover of capital rather than to produce an additional return on capital 'lent' to a customer. Make sure your method:

- recovers the cost of extending credit
- gives the customer the greatest continuing incentive to pay promptly.

6. Consider carefully the following self-testing questions on credit

Policy
- Is there one person in your firm who is ultimately responsible for supervising credit and for ensuring the prompt collection of monies due and who is accountable if the credit position gets out of hand? The exercise of their authority should not detract from the individual salesperson's relationship with the customer – nor from the individual salesperson's

responsibility for seeing that the sales which they make are paid for in accordance with the firm's credit terms.

- Do you have a clear-cut maximum credit policy? Is it written down? Is it known to all your sales staff? Are they instructed to ensure that all your customers are familiar with your policy?
- Are you clear in your own mind as to how you assess credit risks and how you are to impose normal limits – both in terms of total indebtedness for each customer's open account (including cheques in course of collection) and also in terms of time?

Bad debts

- Do you recognise that – assuming you make 1.5 per cent net sales – a loss of £1,500 in bad debts nullifies the net profit on £100,000 sales and destroys all the effort involved in making those sales?
- Do you recognise that an avoidable loss of £1,500 in bad debts means that a lot of abortive effort will have been expended in trying to collect this money before it is written off – and that the cost of this effort is probably 'hidden' and never identified?
- Do you recognise on the other hand that the absence of any doubtful – as opposed to bad – debts probably means that you have been missing out on business by being 'overcautious'?

Granting or extending credit

- Do you methodically check the financial standing of all new customers before executing the first order?
- Do you re-check the financial standing of existing customers whose purchases have recently shown a substantial increase?
- Do you use the telephone when checking trade references? Suppliers will often tell you over the telephone what they would not put in writing.
- Do you recognise that salesmen are by nature optimists? Do you therefore rely on other sources of information before establishing (or increasing) credit facilities for customers?

Credit control and collection

- How soon do your invoices go out after the goods are dispatched? Can this be speeded up?
- How soon do monthly statements go out following the last day of the month? Can this be speeded up?
- Are the terms of sale clearly and precisely shown on all quotations, price lists, invoices and statements?
- What is the actual average length of credit you are giving – or your customers are taking? What length of credit do you allow?
- Do you prepare monthly lists of all customers whose settlement is overdue and do you list the total indebtedness of slow customers as well as the overdue amount? If their slow paying habits reflect financial difficulties, the whole debt may be at risk.

- Do you have a collection procedure timetable? Do you stick to it?
- Are you politely firm but insistent in your collection routine?
- Do you watch the ratio of total debt on balances on the Sales Ledger at the end of each month in relation to the sales of the immediately preceding twelve months? Is the position improving, deteriorating, or static? Why?
- Do your salespeople recognise that 'It's not sold until it's paid for'?

Useful reading

Financial management for the small business: the Daily Telegraph guide, 3rd ed, Colin Barrow, London: Kogan Page, 1995

Barclays guide to financial management for the small business, Peter Wilson, Oxford: Basil Blackwell, 1990

Controlling Costs

This checklist is for managers (or owners of small businesses) who wish to address the issue of cost control.

In today's increasingly competitive business environment, getting the most from existing resources whilst ensuring costs do not escalate is one of the keys to business success or failure.

It is important to note, however, that controlling costs does not equate to cutting costs. Although there will always be occasions when a period of belt-tightening is required, frequent cost-cutting can have an adverse effect on the business – product quality may be affected so alienating customers, relationships with suppliers may be affected and staff may be demoralised. Inappropriate signals concerning the health of the business may also be made.

MCI Standards

This checklist has relevance for the MCI Management Standards: Key Role B – Manage Resources.

Definition

A cost is the value of that which must be given up to acquire or achieve something.

Costs are the price paid for the acquisition, processing and delivery activities of turning raw materials into finished goods.

Costs may also be known as overheads or expenses – the term cost will be used throughout this checklist.

Advantages of controlling costs

- Cost control can provide essential management information.
- Effective cost control is an indicator of good management practice.
- Cost data is the basis on which a pricing structure can be formulated.

Action checklist

1. Collect data on costs incurred

In order to implement cost control within an organisation, it is essential to collect data on what the costs actually are. Costs are often broadly categorised as labour costs, materials costs and general overheads. It is usually assumed that labour costs in service organisations are the greatest percentage of the total; in manufacturing however, figures are more likely to be: labour costs 15%, materials costs 50% and general overheads 30%.

2. Communicate cost awareness

Financial strategies must be communicated to, shared with and owned by all employees so that they understand the financial implications of their activities and decisions. It is important that employees are aware of the full costs of their activities as well as alternatives to them. For example telephone and stationery billing may be centralised, although true costing of all products and services should take account of this overhead on a departmental or activity basis.

Where the activities of cost centres are left unattributed, the level of service usage of such a centre should be considered in the cost allocation process.

3. Examine cost-allocation processes

The budget is the keenest instrument of cost control in any organisation. Drawing up and controlling a budget are covered in separate checklists. Budget control is a self-evident factor in cost control, but there are additional approaches and techniques which can support this process.

One method of discovering true costs is to re-start the budgeting process from scratch and attempt to estimate – as if there were a blank sheet of paper – the full costs of an activity. This is called zero-based budgeting, and works on the basis that annual budget allocations should be justified from the ground upwards. Discovering full cost allocation in this way may well prompt the question: 'Is this activity necessary in the first place?' Remember fixed costs. If you take an activity out, then an element of fixed cost will be re-allocated to the remaining activities.

Activity-based costing (ABC) involves looking closely at those key factors that influence an organisation's overheads and attempts to work out what constitute the key cost factors. ABC requires that all costs associated with a product – from research and new product development to marketing and delivery – should be identified as product costs, or split up and traced to individual products or services.

Costs, however, are often difficult to isolate, because they are made up of multiple tasks and activities which may appear unrelated in the structure of the organisation. For example, we receive a service from another section or department, and are aware of its value to us, but unaware of the cost attached to its supply. One method of tackling this is Overhead Value Analysis, which attempts to trace and quantify the workflows – increasingly these are information workflows – which take place in the supply of services to other parts of the organisation.

4. Identify the various cost elements

Costs are either fixed, such as buildings, or variable, such as raw materials. Some costs fall in between; these are known as semi-variable.

Major cost elements include:

- space, rental, local business tax
- energy costs, such as heating and lighting, as well as the costs of waste, disposal and possible pollution. Is there an environmental policy in force?
- staff costs including salaries and wages – and not forgetting the costs of recruitment, absenteeism, sick pay, pensions and insurance
- raw materials and services bought in
- travel and transport – have new telecommunications technologies been considered?
- general costs of communication – postage, telephone, fax, stationery and supplies – email as an alternative?
- security and insurance – without turning a disaster into a crisis, can you be without them? Are there preferable services rates worth investigating? Is there a disaster recovery plan?
- costs of borrowing, of allowing credit, and of bad debts.

5. Monitor variable costs

Variable costs are normally tied to sales volume. They may include:

- salaries and wages
- advertising costs
- selling expenses
- mailing expenses
- stationery supplies
- subscriptions
- heat, light, power and water.

What is the continuing relationship between sales volume and costs? Is the trend healthy or unhealthy, positive or negative?

6. Examine your costs and expenses regularly

Recognise that effective control can help you to increase your profits on the same or even a reduced volume of sales – or of turnover. Keep the pattern of your sales volume over time as closely under observation as your costs. Know the reasons for abnormal increases or decreases.

Calculate regularly the costs of goods sold as a percentage of net sales. Look for increases or decreases in the price of purchased items, increased transport costs, wastage, or losses due to theft.

Do not let your fixed costs blindly follow increases in sales volume which may not be repeated.

7. Be aware of how cost control affects other components of profitability

Remember that costs are only one member of the family of factors which together influence profitability. The others are:

- sales volume/value
- net margins
- capital employed
- product mix.

A change in any one affects each of the others, favourably or unfavourably. If cost control leads to a dramatic change in costs, then be mindful of the likely impact on sales volume, net margins, capital employed, and product mix. You cannot always have your cake and eat it.

8. Remember quality

Remember the primacy of the customer, whose own personal loyalty is to the best quality at the lowest price. Buying in the cheapest raw materials is not usually the best solution, as cheaper often means worse not better.

Schemes such as TQM, ISO9000 and continuous improvement programmes to improve quality in organisations bear evidence of capability to reduce costs through systematic removal of waste and duplication, largely by empowering the workforce and pushing decisions down to where the work is actually done.

Dos and don'ts for controlling costs

Do

- Re-examine your costs and expenses regularly.
- Recognise that it is easier to exercise control 'before' rather than correct 'after'.
- Keep financial reporting systems up-to-date and publish financial targets regularly.
- Issue key statistics to managers and keep all staff informed.

Don't

- Forget that staff may have useful views on controllable costs.
- Overlook the fact that cost control may have an impact on staff morale – which may be good or bad.

Useful reading

Cost control: a strategic guide, David Doyle, London: Kogan Page and the Chartered Institute of Management Accountants, 1994

How to control your costs and increase your profits: over 400 practical cost control ideas, David M Martin, Hemel Hempstead: Director Books in association with the Institute of Directors, 1992

Overhead cost, John Innes and Falconer Mitchell, London: Academic Press in association with the Chartered Institute of Management Accountants, 1993

Measuring the cost of capacity, Hamilton, Ontario; The Society of Management Accountants of Canada, 1996

How to cut your business costs, Peter D Brunt, London: Kogan Page, 1988

Thought starters

- Do you know the full costs of workflow processes in your organisation?
- What discounts do you receive? Why?
- Does your budgeting process account for inter-related, hidden costs?
- Do you involve staff in problem-solving?

Controlling Credit

This checklist deals with the control of credit allowed to customers and clients for goods and services. Credit control is a vital component in the process of controlling cash flow. Many companies have failed in the past because management did not distinguish between profitability and cash flow. An otherwise profitable enterprise can fail if it runs out of readily available funds with which to meet its commitments and failure to control credit is a frequent cause of this situation. The supplier's funds are being used to finance customers' or clients' businesses rather than the business of the supplier. The granting of excessive credit, whether in terms of amount or of duration, can also have an impact on profit, even if funds are readily available.

MCI Standards

This checklist has relevance for the MCI Management Standards: Key Role B – Manage Resources.

Definition

Allowing customers and clients to defer payment for goods and services is a common and often necessary practice. Credit control is the totality of the policies, procedures and practices which ensure that the total amount of credit extended and the period for which it is extended are consistent with the organisation's policy. These will include ensuring that credit is granted on a systematic basis; the costs of extending credit are adequately recovered; the customer or client continues to pay within the agreed terms; and the need for access to liquid funds is achieved.

Remember: 'It's not sold until it's paid for!'

Benefits of credit control

Credit control:

- prevents bad debts
- plays a major part in the control of cash flow
- contributes to improved returns on capital and net profit
- may make the difference between an enterprise's ability or inability to grow

- may be the key factor in an enterprise's ability to survive in times of difficulty.

Problems with credit control

Credit control:

- is time consuming
- may lead to difficult relations with customers and clients who have become accustomed to receiving uncontrolled credit
- may leave an enterprise operating below maximum capacity
- may result, in extreme cases, in fixed costs being unrecovered.

None of these 'disadvantages', however, provides a good reason for not controlling credit.

Action checklist

1. Assign responsibility for credit control

Ensure that one person in your organisation, at a suitably senior level, is ultimately responsible for negotiating, granting and supervising credit and for ensuring the prompt collection of monies due. Appoint someone who can supervise the Credit Controller and can be accountable if the credit position becomes questionable. The exercise of this authority should not detract from the relationships with customers and clients of individual members of staff, especially specialist sales staff. The latter still have a responsibility for ensuring that sales are made and goods and services paid for in accordance with the firm's terms and conditions.

2. Introduce a credit policy

Introduce a clear cut maximum credit policy – covering both amount and duration of credit. Write it down so it cannot be changed arbitrarily. Be sure that it is known to all your staff who may be involved in granting credit. Be sure also that customers and clients are informed about your policy.

3. Re-examine terms of sale

Re-examine all quotations, price-lists, invoices, statements and similar documents which you issue. Do they show the terms on which you do business, especially the terms on which you grant credit? Don't be afraid of telling potential customers and clients your terms. If you are serious about credit control, they must know sooner or later. The chances are that they will respect you as a supplier with a businesslike approach rather than as one 'making up the rules as the game progresses', or, worse still, having no rules at all. Be aware that contracts are established and modified by each successive piece of paper prior to invoice. Care needs to be taken to ensure that your credit terms are not replaced by those of a customer or client as detailed on their order document.

4. Assess credit risks

Be clear in your own mind how you assess credit risks for new and existing customers and clients and how you impose limits in terms of a customer or client's indebtedness and in terms of time. Satisfy yourself that you and your staff do this in a systematic way and that the potential volume of turnover which a customer or client may offer is not a factor which you take into account. Recognise that salesmen are optimists by nature – especially if commission is involved. Pursue other sources of information before increasing or establishing credit facilities for existing or potential customers or clients. Sources might include trade and bank references, credit agencies and rating registers (Dun and Bradstreet for example), trade sources and your competitors, and online sources.

5. Recheck existing customers and clients

Recheck the financial standing of all customers and clients on a regular basis and also when purchases show a sudden substantial increase. Satisfy yourself that the increase is due to successful selling rather than to a competitor ceasing to supply – perhaps because of problems in securing payment.

6. Recognise the effect of bad debts

Recognise that bad debts reduce bottom line profits and destroy all the effort made in reaching the much larger value of sales required to generate those profits. Recognise also that any bad debt means that much abortive effort will have been expended in trying to collect this money before it was written off and that the cost of this effort is probably 'hidden' and never identified. If you have no doubtful – as opposed to bad – debts, recognise that you may have been missing out on profitable business by being over-cautious.

7. Review the invoicing process and the issue of monthly statements

The date on which a customer receives an invoice or statement will often determine when they will make payment. Take a fresh look at the interval between the supply of goods and services and the submission of invoices. See whether the process cannot be speeded up – it probably can.
Likewise find out how soon monthly statements go out after the last day of the month. Ask yourself, honestly, whether their preparation and dispatch is being deferred to enable some work of lesser priority to be done.

8. List overdue and total indebtedness

You should prepare an Aged Debtors Analysis, which is a monthly list of all those whose settlement is overdue. List their total indebtedness as well as the overdue amount analysed by the month in which payment was due. If slow paying habits reflect financial difficulties, the whole debt may be at risk.

9. Monitor the average length of credit

Calculate the average length of credit which your business is allowing – or which your customers or clients are taking. This can be calculated monthly, quarterly or even annually but ideally a monthly figure should be extracted. The only thing worse than bad news is bad news which arrives too late for remedial action.

The calculation required is:

$$\frac{\text{Total outstanding debtor balances at month end (the amount you are owed in total)}}{\text{Sales value for 12 months period ending at the same month end}} \times 365 = \begin{array}{c}\text{Average number} \\ \text{of days credit} \\ \text{you are allowing}\end{array}$$

For example, if you divide your total outstanding debtor balances of £10,000 by the sales value for the 12 month period of £100,000 and multiply that by 365, you find that you are allowing an average 36.5 days credit to each debtor.

Establish this calculation as a regular routine. Remember to adjust the annual sales value each time you make the calculation by deducting the sales value for the most remote month and adding the most recent figure. Keep a very simple graph which will show you whether the average period for which you are allowing credit is increasing or decreasing. The graph will look like this:

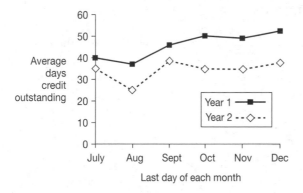

Look for any movement between the end of one month and the end of the next AND look for the trend revealed by the graph as a whole. This particular approach will emphasise length of credit being allowed or taken rather than the amount. Both time and amount are relevant to profit and to liquidity.

10. Introduce a collection procedure

If you do not have a collection procedure timetable introduce one. If you do have a timetable, check whether it is systematically followed. Be politely firm in your collection routines. Remember to always record details of any telephone calls, including dates and the names of people talked to. Attempt to get clear commitment to dates and amounts of payments.

Dos and don'ts for controlling credit

Do

- Have a clear vision of what you require from credit control.
- Remember that a businesslike approach is attractive to the right type of customer or client.
- Regard the control of credit as a vital regular check on the financial health of your business.

Don't

- Let credit control dominate everything else.
- Allow the volume of sales to influence your view of credit-worthiness.
- Make excuses for bad payers – leave that to them.

Useful reading

Successful credit control in a week, Roger Mason, London: Hodder & Stoughton, 1998
Ready drafted credit control letters and forms, Russell W Bell, Hemel Hempstead: Director Books, 1992
Credit management, 3rd ed, R M V Bass, Cheltenham: Stanley Thornes, 1991
Successful credit control, Martin Posner, Oxford: BSP Professional Books, 1990

Thought starters

- How does the length of credit you receive compare with the length of credit you allow?
- What incentive to pay promptly do your customers or clients have?
- If they only deal with you because of the credit you allow, it doesn't say much for your goods or services, does it?

Collecting Debts

This checklist deals with the question of debt collection and should be used in conjunction with the checklist on Controlling Credit.

All businesses which operate on the basis of extending credit to customers and clients will, from time to time, be faced with the situation when payment is overdue. At what point extended credit becomes a debt to be collected and how urgently is a matter for individual decision. This checklist outlines sound principles for action from that point onwards.

MCI Standards

This checklist has relevance for the MCI Management Standards: Key Role B – Manage Resources.

Definition

Debt collection is the generic name for the processes and procedures adopted by organisations which have extended credit for goods and services to customers or clients and then find that payment is overdue, or not forthcoming spontaneously.

Action checklist

1. Remember that prevention is better than cure

Think about the possible steps which may be taken to minimise the possibility of bad debts. Decide who will operate your policy. Some of the options include:

- a factoring agency
- a lawyer or agency who provides access to standard stationery
- your own staff – either dedicated exclusively to debt collection, or part of the accounts control or credit team.

Most debt collection practice requires a mixture of approaches. Remember that all your staff who are in contact with customers or clients need to contribute to the process of collecting payments.

2. Think of needs inside the organisation

There will be a need for:

- systems which detect arrears and potential bad debts early
- good communication and understanding between departments, especially sales, accounts, credit control and debt collection
- staff with procedural knowledge and good interpersonal skills
- regular review of policies, procedures and criteria for granting or extending credit
- firmly applied policies with regular reviews to ensure that debt collection procedures are implemented immediately if they are appropriate
- regular training or refreshers in interpersonal skills, procedural and attitudinal practices, for example, in developing both a persistent and sympathetic manner.

3. Concentrate on big debts

Remember that 20% of your debtors probably account for 80% of the debt outstanding at any one time. An even smaller percentage is involved in bad, or potentially bad, debts. Pursue the big debts first and remember that, while it may be easier to collect the smaller sums which are overdue, this may not necessarily be the best approach. The effectiveness of debt collection should be assessed by the amount of money recovered and not by the number of debts collected. Bear in mind, however, that:

- several smaller debts can add up to one large debt
- for a large debt a phone call before it falls due may be appropriate
- for a small debt the process may start with a letter one month after payment is due
- debts are seldom as simple as a single invoice or one month's transactions – they usually involve many transactions with invoices and credit notes over several months.

4. Write positive letters

Recognise that in the first instance an approach by letter is cheaper than approaching your debtors by telephone. Be sure that your letters are courteous, clear, specific and addressed to a named executive.

Be firm, concise and unwavering. Do not include an apology, suggest compromise or refer to the possibility of part-payment. Do not avoid the issue of payment now by asking for reasons for non-payment rather than for payment. Recognise that an excuse is no substitute for your money. Understand that if you make threats you must be prepared to carry them out if you do not wish to lose credibility.

Having pursued a debt by letter, re-apply your control of credit procedure before extending further credit. Consider putting all business on a deposit in advance or cash on delivery (COD) basis until you receive payment and can satisfy your conditions for the granting of credit.

For maximum impact ensure that your letters appear to have been individually prepared. To show individuality and demonstrate the close monitoring of debts make reference to previous letters, quoting dates.

Avoid the use of the word 'first', such as 'first demand'. 'First' implies 'second' or more to follow – don't give the debtor another reason to delay payment. Avoid the use of 'final' unless you mean it. Be polite, be brief and be firm. Give the debtor a better reason for paying than for not paying. For example:

- offer an opportunity to protect the debtor's reputation
- point out the advantages of continuing to trade together
- point out the advantages of enjoying – but not abusing – credit terms, and of ensuring their continued availability
- suggest that payment will ensure that third parties do not become involved
- express the hope that legal action can be avoided.

Many organisations have a series of three or four letters with escalation in tone and authority. In order to provide proof for any potential legal proceedings, these need to be issued regardless of any other courses of action.

5. Follow up letters by using the telephone if appropriate and necessary

The telephone is an essential tool in collecting payments. You should not underestimate, however, the cost and time commitment involved with telephone calls. Before calling the debtor be fully prepared. Have available all files, copies of invoices, and:

- the debtor's correct name and legal status
- the name of the person you need to talk to
- the amount, date and full details of the debt
- the agreed terms and conditions of the sale or supply
- details of previous communications, if any
- the date of the last payment (if any) received
- how you will respond to excuses, requests for more time to pay and requests for acceptance of part payment.

Having contacted the right person, give your name and personalise the discussion. Recognise the need for persuasive skills to gain commitment, to convert interest into action and to find out reasons for the delay – they may be relevant to the future generation of credit. Find out, if you can, whether a query, dispute, financial problem or oversight lies behind the delay in payment. If you are told 'a cheque is in the post', press for details.

When was the cheque sent, where from, and what were its date and number? If it was not for the full amount outstanding, why?

If the debtor fails to honour a promise made on the telephone, you will need to consider what further actions to take. Likewise, if you cannot gain access after several attempts to the person to whom you wish to speak, escalate the debt recovery chain.

6. Remember the fax as a variant to a letter

Note that a fax message gives a sense of immediacy and that faxed messages tend to be dealt with more quickly than letters. Remember that the content may be more public within the debtor's organisation – those concerned may be embarrassed into payment. A fax or email may be sent direct to the desk of the recipient and therefore gain immediate attention.

7. All else having failed, consider visiting the debtor

Visiting is the least cost-effective method of collection; it is difficult for those who wish to avoid confrontation, and you may feel that you have lost face if you leave without a cheque. If you decide to visit the debtor, arrive unexpectedly, be firm, courteous and unwavering and, if you do not collect a cheque, move quickly to the next stage.

8. Appoint a debt collection agency

Use only those agencies registered with the Office of Fair Trading and which have a good reputation. Don't pay the agency 'up front' or agree to a flat fee. Agree only to pay a percentage of what the agency recovers. Obtain a banker's reference and talk to other users of the agency. Be sure that you know the agency's terms and conditions and that they are acceptable to you.

9. Think before you instruct solicitors or become involved in litigation

Remember that solicitors are expensive and require payment whether or not they achieve results – seek advice and a price before any commitment. Litigation is even more expensive. Be sure, before you start, that the debtor has money with which to pay, that you have reasonable evidence of the existence of the debt and that the debt is less than six years old. Be sure that you have the full name and address and legal status of the debtor.

10. Don't return a post-dated cheque without thought

A post-dated cheque is better than no cheque. It may be paid if presented. It provides proof of debt if the bank does not pay the cheque. Consider carefully, however, whether you want to continue trading on the basis of post-dated cheques.

Be aware of the dangers of being charged with harassment, for example by threatening violence, damaging property or breaking and entering. Know that you must not make such demands of your debtors as to cause either them or their families concern, distress or humiliation, either by their nature or their frequency. Remember that you must not represent yourself as having some official capacity with authority to enforce payment.

Dos and don'ts for collecting debts

Do

- Know your customers – customer knowledge can help to prevent rather than cure.
- Remember the effort that went into making the sale for which you have not been paid.
- Consider the consequences of not being paid.

Don't

- Start your collection process by offering compromise
- Forget that it's your money you are chasing – not theirs.

Useful reading

BOOKS

Successful credit control in a week, Roger Mason, London: Hodder & Stoughton, 1998
Ready drafted credit control letters and forms, Russell W Bell, Hemel Hempstead: Director Books in association with the Institute of Directors, 1992
The exporters guide to getting paid, London: Association of British Factors and Discounters, 1993

JOURNAL ARTICLES

What to do when your debtors don't want to pay, Small Business Confidential, October no 146 1995, pp3–5
Get debts paid faster, Gillian Clegg, Small Business Confidential, August no 96 1991, pp4–6

Reading a Balance Sheet

This checklist helps you both to read a balance sheet and to understand the significance of the figures which make it up. It is intended as an outline guide for the general manager, not as a replacement for full accounting support and interpretation.

MCI Standards

This checklist has relevance for the MCI Management Standards: Key Role B – Manage Resources.

Definition

A balance sheet is a financial statement of a company's assets and liabilities, grouped under generic headings, on a given date and is one of the financial statements required under company legislation.

Although a company may produce a balance sheet on any date for its own internal purposes, one must be produced on the last day of the company's financial year for statutory purposes.

The balance sheet is normally set alongside a profit and loss account. It is important to recognise that a balance sheet is compiled on a given date and that the profit and loss account is a summary of all the company's transactions during the period ending on the date of the balance sheet. The balance sheet is a 'snapshot' at a point in time; the profit and loss account is a 'film' of the company's activities over the period in question.

Benefits of understanding a balance sheet

- A view of the company's net worth, and of assets and liabilities on the balance sheet date can be formed.
- A view of the shareholding of the company on the basis of the types of share available, the numbers issued and the relative proportions of the types of share issued, such as preference vs ordinary (preference shares would have a higher ranking than ordinary shares if dividends were to be restricted), can be obtained.
- Used with earlier balance sheets, it indicates how the company is progressing (or not).

Problems with balance sheets

- You may forget that a balance sheet is a 'snapshot' on a given date and that the picture can change radically from one day to the next.
- You may forget that the value of stock is often based on subjective judgement.
- You might overlook the fact that today's healthy debtor may be tomorrow's bad debtor.
- The items listed provide a 'book' value, which may not be an accurate reflection of what they are worth on the open market.
- It does not provide a complete picture of a company's overall performance. Other statements, including the Profit and Loss, and Funds Flow Statements, need to be studied to obtain this.
- It only includes items which have a specific, monetary value, which cannot – by themselves – show the company's real worth. Most published balance sheets are prepared for investors.

Action checklist

1. Examine the fixed assets

Assets are items owned by the company, expressed in financial terms. 'Fixed assets' are those permanent items of long-term use to a business and appear at the top of the balance sheet. These may be divided into three categories:

- tangible – land, buildings, plant, equipment, machinery, fixtures and fittings, motor vehicles
- intangible – licences, intellectual property, patents, goodwill
- investments – in other companies, government stocks.

Fixed assets are likely to be long-term assets and are most likely to be items in which the company does not trade.

2. Look at current assets

'Current' or 'liquid' assets are the ever-changing items which fluctuate as a company goes about its business. These would include:

- short-term investments
- stocks of raw materials
- work in progress
- stocks of finished goods/goods for sale
- stocks of stationery and consumables
- money owed to the company (debtors)
- prepayments (payments made wholly or partially in advance such as rent)
- cash in hand and balances in the bank.

Current assets are likely to be owned by the company for a shorter period (less than a year).

The order of the assets on the balance sheet is usually determined by the ease or difficulty with which they can be turned into ready money. Fixed assets, especially land and buildings, are usually the least liquid. Money is always the most liquid.

3. Look at the current liabilities

On a balance sheet, liabilities are arranged in ascending order of liquidity.

'Current' liabilities are the short-term debts of a company which need to be settled in the next 12 months. These debts might include bank loans and overdrafts, taxes due, VAT, deposits and prepayments (by customers).

4. Look at long-term liabilities

'Long-term' liabilities include loan capital on which interest is paid and which must eventually be repaid. Long-term loans (perhaps secured) follow, and then deferred liabilities (tax perhaps) and creditors (suppliers).

5. Check net current assets

Deducting current liabilities from current assets will leave 'net current assets' – or working capital. Net current assets are added to the fixed amounts to reach a 'net worth' figure, or 'total capital employed'.

6. Read the 'financed by' section

Below or alongside the assets and liabilities will be a section showing how activities have been funded. Normally, these funds will have come from owners' capital, and re-invested profit or surplus from previous years. They could also derive from long-term loans. The total figure will be the same as that for 'net assets'.

7. Consider assets vs liabilities

If the assets exceed the liabilities the difference is known as shareholders' or proprietors' funds. If the liabilities exceed the assets, there is no net worth and the organisation is insolvent and should not be trading. If it is, look out for the personal guarantees or the accommodating bank which may be keeping the organisation in existence.

8. Pause for a moment and think about depreciation and obsolescence

Assets do not have infinite lives. Statute, accounting conventions, good practice and prudence require an allowance called depreciation to be made in the Profit and Loss Account for assets wearing out or becoming obsolete.

Look closely at the fixed assets – they usually show an original value and the amount already written off over the life to-date of the asset, the two giving the current value of the asset, known as its 'written down' or 'book value'. Note that freehold land may actually be appreciating while buildings depreciate, and some more fragile assets lose value on the day after their purchase dates.

There are various methods of calculating depreciation for the year. The most simple, the 'straight line method', is to divide the expected loss in value of the asset over its expected lifetime, by the number of years which make up its expected lifetime. For example, an asset, purchased for £10,000 is expected to be retained for three years and to be disposed of for £7,000. £1,000 will be charged over each of the three years to depreciation. The balance sheet will show written down values in successive years of £9,000, £8,000 and finally £7,000.

For tax purposes, assets are depreciated according to rules laid down by the Inland Revenue authorities.

Stocks are included in a balance sheet at a value which is based on the original cost or market value, whichever is the lower at the time, thus recognising damage, obsolescence, pilferage, or other causes of loss in value.

9. Be aware of ratio analysis

In order to interpret a balance sheet, certain inferences and comparisons will have to be made, and ratios are one method by which this can be achieved.

Financial ratios can be a valuable tool in comparing the balance sheet of one company with that of another. Be wary, however, because there may be major differences in the accounting policies used in different companies; this can make comparison of ratios between organisations misleading.

Rather than company comparison, a safer use of ratio analysis is to analyse trends over time within the same organisation, whereby current asset ratios are monitored over a number of years. An example is the so-called 'quick ratio' – the ratio of current assets to current liabilities.

Caution must be expressed, however, as applying financial ratios to interpret accounts or make projections can be a matter for specialist application.

Dos and don'ts for reading a balance sheet

Do
- Remember that a balance sheet may be valid for only one day.
- Remember that the value of a balance sheet may lie more in what it reveals after analysis than in the actual figures it contains.
- Remember that comparison of carefully selected ratios is the most effective way of comparing two balance sheets.

Don't
- Overlook the Profit and Loss Account and the Funds Flow Statement – the picture is incomplete without them.
- Forget that these are 'paper' or 'book' values and not necessarily what would be obtained if the items were sold.

Useful addresses
Institute of Chartered Accountants in England and Wales, PO Box 433, Chartered Accountants' Hall, Moorgate Place, London EC2P 2BJ, Tel: 0171 920 8100
Institute of Chartered Accountants of Scotland, 27 Queen Street, Edinburgh EH2 1LA, Tel: 0131 225 5673
Institute of Chartered Accountants of Ireland, 87-89 Pembroke Road, Ballsbridge, Dublin 4, Republic of Ireland, Tel: +1 668 0400

Useful reading

BOOKS
Understanding company accounts: the Daily Telegraph guide, 4th ed, Bob Rothenberg and John Newman, London: Kogan Page, 1995
Introduction to annual reports and accounts, Institute of Chartered Accountants in England and Wales and Proshare, London: 1995
Finance for the perplexed executive, Rev ed, Ray Proctor, London: Harper Collins, 1994
Balance sheets basics for nonfinancial managers, Joseph Peter Simini, New York: John Wiley, 1990

JOURNAL ARTICLE
Making sense of the balance sheet, David Sleath, Modern Management Journal, Winter vol 2 no 5 1988, pp18–19

Spotting Fraud

This checklist is about how to spot fraud. The focus is on how an organisation can put simple measures in place to prevent fraud. The underlying idea behind the checklist is that everyone has a role in the process of spotting and preventing fraud.

Fraud has become something of a hot potato over recent years. In part this has been due to the efforts of the Audit Commission and of groups like Public Concern at Work which have highlighted the problem of fraud. The message coming from these organisations is that, in order to spot and prevent fraud, companies need to take it seriously and tackle it on all fronts.

MCI Standards

The checklist has relevance for the MCI Management Standards: Key Role B – Manage Resources.

Definition

The following is based on the Audit Commission definition. Fraud is:

'the intentional distortion of financial statements or other records by persons internal or external to the organisation which is carried out to conceal the misappropriation of assets or otherwise for gain'.

Advantages

There are many obvious advantages to spotting fraud. These include:

- saving money – it has been estimated that fraud costs the private sector alone £9 billion a year
- avoiding damage to morale – no one wants to work for an organisation where fraud is rife and never investigated
- accountability – tackling fraud is one aspect of public accountability.

Disadvantages

If you don't tackle fraud:

- it may become public knowledge and then the organisation can be faced with a PR disaster
- it can affect the confidence of your organsation's funders, shareholders, customers and service users.

Action checklist

The following checklist will help you to spot and tackle fraud. There are two elements to tackling fraud:

- putting systems in place
- putting an anti-fraud culture in place.

Putting systems in place

1. Write a fraud strategy statement

Write guidelines to help answer questions such as:

- when does pilfering become fraud and hospitality or perks become corruption?
- can staff accept any gifts?

Without guiding principles, it is difficult for people to differentiate between what is accepted custom and practice and what is not acceptable. So, set out a strategy on financial malpractice.

Try to develop a separate procedure which spells out clearly:

- who is responsible for dealing with fraud
- the stages involved in raising and dealing with a concern.

2. Set up an audit committee

Establishing an audit committee can be a useful way of setting the framework for fraud control. The committee should consist of senior stakeholders from a range of different departments (people who have influence to make any recommended changes stick and insight into the causes of fraud) and committee members (if your organisation has a committee).

The job of such an audit committee is to:

- help to investigate examples of malpractice and suggest action when they are uncovered

- help to design fraud prevention measures and develop a more effective fraud prevention system
- review the organisation's anti-fraud strategy.

The audit committee can act as a reporting line for an organisation's internal auditor. It acts as a guiding and controlling influence, a policy and strategy forum and a vehicle for accountability.

3. Tighten up anti-fraud procedures

Poorly documented procedures contribute to fraud.

4. Make the most of information technology

Organisations often hold vast amounts of information, and in particular, financial information. Fraudsters often perpetrate their crimes because one department does not know what the others are doing – this may give them the chance to carry out multiple fraud. Integrated and relational databases enable organisations to cross-reference information – internally and indeed with other organisations. So use information technology to share information and thus spot fraud where it is occurring. Many local authorities use IT to help share information about people who claim multiple housing benefit. This has proved a highly effective weapon against fraudsters.

5. Establish good relations with the police

Work with the police and the Crown Prosecution Service to establish exactly what is necessary to give the police the opportunity to obtain a conviction. Set clear guidelines for managers to tell them how to conduct an internal investigation and at what stage they should involve the police.

6. Establish procedures for effective fraud investigation

The following is based on a good practice checklist for effective fraud investigations:

- identify a steering officer for each investigation
- contact the police at an early stage and keep them informed
- consider the likely outcomes, ie prosecution, or internal disciplinary action
- agree the target dates and key issues
- identify who will carry out the investigation
- hold steering meetings to discuss progress, agree variations and identify future targets
- identify the actions required.

Putting an anti-fraud culture in place

Creating the right environment to tackle fraud needs a range of initiatives, some of which are difficult to evaluate but important nonetheless. In many organisations there is a good deal of apparently trivial fraud which is accepted as the norm. Changing this perception, and changing this practice, can be difficult, and cause some resentment.

1. Leadership from managers

Any initiative aimed at openness is only as good as its leaders. It is likely that there may be some cynicism from staff about any new approach. They may well have had experience of concerns being brushed under the carpet in the past. The message about fraud and corruption needs to come clearly from the top and be reinforced with action.

2. Make communication work

Involve your employees, listen to their sense of right and wrong. Explain what fraud is and the effect it has on their jobs and the services they provide to their customers (both internal and external).

- Make it known how seriously you treat the problem.
- If it is fraud, call it fraud when you find it.
- Use seminars, newsletters and briefing sessions to explain your commitment to tackling fraud and to report on your successes.

3. Other anti-fraud training

Any new system needs to be reinforced with training. You can use training to stress your key messages about fraud and the need for vigilance and openness and to explain the way the system works. More importantly, training can also help to instil new coaching and counselling skills that managers will need to handle concerns effectively.

4. Open up routes

It is important to open up routes through which concerns about fraud can be channelled. Apart from line managers, staff need the option of another route to raise their concerns. This could be the Chief Executive or finance officer, an employee in internal audit or another named senior manager in a larger business.

There should be a clearly identified and easily accessible route to this person, such as a hotline.

A final word

The measures above are suggestions. You may already do many of the things mentioned. The key is to keep a balance between the procedures and guidelines and to work at developing a feedback culture.

Dos and don'ts for spotting fraud

Do
- Take fraud seriously.
- Define it clearly.
- Set up a system to deal with it.
- Reinforce key messages about fraud for senior managers.
- Act and be seen to act when you uncover fraud.

Don't
- Brush fraud under the carpet.
- Be soft on it.
- Block your ears to the concerns of staff – they are the ones who are most likely to spot fraud.
- Just put a system in place without working on the softer culture issues.

Useful reading

BOOKS
Fraudbusting: how to identify and deal with corporate fraud and how to prevent it, David Price, London: Mercury Books, 1991
Fraud – how to fight it, London: Arthur Young, 1987

JOURNAL ARTICLES
Your company is being defrauded, Mike Yuille, Management Today, March 1998, pp 60–62, 64
Fraud control: best practice in business, George McKillop and Malcolm Shackell, Australian Accountant, Vol 67 no 9, October 1997, pp 46, 48–49
Dirty rotten scoundrels, Ray Mgadzah, Human Resources UK, No 30, May / June 1997, pp 44–45, 47–48

Useful addresses
Public Concern at Work, Suite 306, 16 Baldwins Gardens, London, EC1N 7RJ, Tel: 0171 404 6609

Thought starters

- Have you clearly defined what fraud is?
- Are you an organisation that listens to concerns?
- Are your anti-fraud procedures clear and thought through?
- Have you developed strong links with the police?

Using Management Consulting Services Effectively

This checklist is for prospective users of consultants and suggests some of the questions they should ask themselves before approaching a consultant to undertake an assignment. There is little doubt that calling on the service of a management consultant can often prove to be a valuable investment provided:

- you allow enough time for the whole exercise

- the problem area has been carefully defined

- you know what you want the consultant to do, having identified all the necessary steps for the task in hand

- care is exercised in selecting the right consultant

- you measure progress towards a solution.

MCI Standards

This checklist has relevance for the MCI Management Standards: Key Role B – Manage Resources.

Definition

'Management consulting is an advisory service contracted for and provided to organisations by specially trained and qualified persons who assist, in an objective and independent manner, the client organisation to identify management problems, analyse such problems, recommend solutions to these problems, and help, when requested, in the implementation of solutions.' **Consulting to management** by Larry E Greiner and Robert O Metzger, Prentice Hall 1983.

Advantages of using consultants

- **Expertise.** Since consultants are immersed in their specialism, they are well-placed to advise on the state of the art. It may be impossible for an organisation to tap such expertise in any other way.
- **Short-term projects.** It may be more cost-effective for a company to buy in skills as and when they are needed.
- **Extra resources.** Help can be required for an overstretched management team or to pursue a project that would otherwise not be completed.
- **Independent viewpoint.** An outsider can see things which are unclear to those on the inside or say things which members of staff may fear to articulate. Equally, employees may be more willing to agree to a course of action if they know that impartial advice has been taken.

Disadvantages of using consultants

- They may be expensive. The Management Consultancy Information Service (see Useful addresses) publishes regular surveys which give a guide to fee rates.
- The end result may be unsatisfactory although steps in the following action checklist will help you to guard against this.
- The work may be left to junior consultancy staff once the assignment starts or personnel may change during the project.
- There may be resentment from staff at the employment of consultants.

Action checklist

1. Involve senior management from the beginning

Gain their approval for the decision to use consultants and keep them informed during the selection process. This will help ensure that your choice of consultant will be accepted at the top level.

2. Gain an awareness of the number and scope of management consulting firms

Some offer a wide range of services, whilst there are others which specialise in particular industries, certain areas of business activity or smaller or larger organisations.

3. Prepare a short list of possible consultants

There are a number of directories and registers available for identifying consultants but recommendation is also commonly used. Make sure you obtain references from previous clients to establish a consultant's track record.

4. Ask for a preliminary survey from consultants on your short list

This should be free, although in certain circumstances a nominal charge may be made. It should enable you to establish the extent to which the consultant can help you, the likely benefits, and the duration of the job. It should also help you to study the consultant's approach to the problem and to your organisation. Ask for a written report of the survey.

5. Study the consultancy proposals submitted

These should have the following common features:

- an understanding of the situation or need
- a programme of work
- an indication of the consultant's management style and approach
- a timetable to accomplish the work
- details of staff involved, including relevant qualifications and experience
- the resources required, such as time, information and equipment
- estimates of fees and costs
- a summary of the results and benefits to be achieved from the project.

6. Explain to all concerned why a consultant is being employed

All relevant staff concerned must be fully briefed on why a consultant has been appointed, when he or she will arrive, and the cooperation that is required. Appoint someone as the main contact with the consultant.

7. Ask for regular reports on the progress of the assignment

Measure actual progress against the agreed objectives of the assignment. Ensure that your requirements are not being shrouded by consultant preferences.

8. Have a debriefing session before the end of the consultancy

Make sure the consultant summarises the findings and conclusions of the project either in a report or in a presentation. Ensure there are no misunderstandings or errors.

9. Assess consultant effectiveness

Check that the new development and procedures proposed are being implemented and properly applied, and that they are not being undermined by old methods and concepts. Discuss with staff concerned any particular difficulties which arise during implementation. Regularly examine the results being achieved and insist on follow-up visits from the consultant at appropriate intervals after completion of the project.

Dos and don'ts for using management consultants

Do

- Invest time in the whole process.
- Have a clear understanding of what you want to achieve.
- Prepare a checklist of requirements as a basis for reducing your short list to the final selection.
- Ensure effective communication and coordination between consultant and staff.

Don't

- Assume that you necessarily need to bring in an outsider.
- Accept friendly recommendations without investigating past performance.
- Presume that staff will readily accept an outside expert.
- Lose sight of your most important objectives.
- Become overly reliant on a consultant.

Useful reading

BOOKS

Directory of management consultants in the UK 1998, 13th ed, Alex Kaminsky, ed., London: AP Information Services, 1997

Getting the most from consultants: a manager's guide to choosing and using consultants, Martin Wilson and the Institute of Management Foundation, London: Pitman, 1996

JOURNAL ARTICLES

Using management consultants, IRS Employment Review, no 620, November 1996, pp7–12

The ten best ways of using management consultants, Geoff Kitts, Human Resources UK, no 15, Autumn 1994, pp19–20, 22, 24, 26

How to select an external consultant, Alan Fowler, Personnel Management Plus, vol 5 no 2, February 1994, pp26–27

Useful addresses

Institute of Management Consultants, 5th Floor, 32-33 Hatton Garden, London EC1N 8DL, Tel: 0171 242 2140; 0800 318030 (Client support service)

British Consultants Bureau, 1 Westminster Palace Gardens, 1-7 Artillery Row, London SW1P 1RJ, Tel: 0171 222 3651

Management Consultancies Association Ltd, 11 West Halkin Street, London SW1X 8JL, Tel: 0171 235 3897

Management Consultancy Information Service, 38 Blenheim Avenue, Gants Hill, Ilford, Essex IG2 6JQ, Tel: 0181 554 4695

All Business Links will provide help for those considering using a consultancy.

Thought starters

- Can you define clearly the problem or issue that needs to be tackled?
- Are you sure the expertise needed is not available internally?
- Have you worked with a consultant before? What was the outcome?

Effective Purchasing

This checklist is designed to assist those responsible for purchasing to adopt a more effective strategy. It is not intended that this checklist should itemise the steps in the administration of a purchase order process; rather it is aimed at presenting a proactive approach to purchasing. Whilst directed at those involved in centralised purchasing, the principles apply equally to decentralised buying.

MCI Standards

This checklist has relevance for the MCI Management Standards: Key Role B – Manage Resources.

Definition

Most textbooks advocate that purchasing is about buying the right goods, at the right time, at the right price, in the right quantity and of the right quality. Whilst this is indeed a fundamental requirement, effective purchasing has to deliver more than this. Adopting an effective purchasing strategy will turn a reactive buyer into a proactive buyer, one who adds value to the process.

Advantages of effective purchasing

It:

- is proactive and adds value for your organisation
- improves communication with suppliers
- provides better understanding of the marketplace.

Disadvantages of effective purchasing

There are no real disadvantages to effective purchasing, but it must be remembered that time must be invested in:

- gathering and sorting internal data
- evaluating suppliers.

Action checklist – Your organisation

1. Understand your own organisation

Take time to learn about how your own organisation functions and what is important to each department in terms of the supply of goods and services. What are the most crucial aspects for each line manager in terms of quality, price and delivery? Which items do they purchase most often and what are they used for? How does each department determine its re-order levels? Gather as much data as you can to provide a sound basis for formulating your strategy. It will also serve to demonstrate professionalism to your internal customers and increase their sense of involvement in the process.

2. Compile a purchase history

Use purchase orders and requisitions to compile a history of purchases. Gather data on product types, order quantities, lead times, pricing, order frequency, etc. Use this data to produce a pattern of purchasing for key items.

3. Use the purchase history to become a proactive buyer

Negotiate better deals with suppliers by giving them an indication of the volumes they can expect over the year. Anticipate re-order dates and do the groundwork in advance. Reduce delivery charges by ordering like products at the same time. Arrange for suppliers to stock frequently used items free of charge, thus reducing your storage requirements, controlling lead times and giving the benefit of bulk purchasing. Monitor price fluctuations for seasonal trends.

Action checklist – Your suppliers

1. Evaluate potential suppliers

Check:

- turnover and profitability
- how long they have been trading
- who their major customers are (if they are reliant on one major customer what will happen to the business if they lose that account?)
- what percentage of their turnover your business will generate
- whether they have any third party certification, such as ISO 9000
- their quality control policy
- their procedure for handling customer complaints
- their invoicing and administrative procedures
- their level of insurance cover.

2. Visit potential suppliers

Find out who would be dealing with your order and how it would be processed. Ask to meet the people with whom you will have day-to-day contact. Are you made to feel welcome?

3. Assess supplier competence

Take up references. Try to talk to buyers in organisations which are similar to your own with similar accounts.

4. Audit your major suppliers

Perform regular audits on your suppliers to assess their continued level of performance. Do they still meet the criteria you established when placing the first order? What improvements have you noticed in the service since then?

5. Maintain good communication

You expect your suppliers to keep you advised of delivery dates and any problems associated with your order. Ensure that you reciprocate – advise them if you are expecting a sudden decrease in purchases or indeed an increased requirement. Just as you should tell them exactly what you want of them, get them to tell you precisely what they expect of you.

Show an interest in your supplier's other business. Have they won or lost any major contracts? How are they affected by the economy? Will transport costs increase as a result of rising fuel prices? Will the price of paper materially affect your major print job scheduled for the end of the year – can you pre-purchase the paper to minimise the effect? Good communication and understanding of your supplier's business will ultimately filter back into your own.

Get to know your suppliers as human beings. It is much easier to deal with matters (especially tricky ones) when you know the person at the other end of the phone (but don't let personal considerations outweigh organisational ones).

6. Use your supplier's expertise

You cannot be an expert in everything. Use your supplier's expertise and knowledge to help you draw up specifications of work.

7. Maintain a competitive element

Always review the price and service you are getting from your supplier. Let them know they have to remain competitive. For audit purposes retain documentation which shows you sought alternative prices.

8. Compare quotations

Ensure quotes are based on a level playing field. Check the exclusions such as delivery, installation, training and insurance. Check the contract period, renewal dates and how long the price is held for. What provision is made to hold prices at current level or within the realms of RPI for long term contracts? What are the payment terms?

9. Visit trade exhibitions

Visiting trade exhibitions and reading trade journals are fundamental to keeping up-to-date with the marketplace and what is on offer.

10. Negotiate when the price must rise

Try to negotiate other advantages, such as longer payment terms, prompt payment discounts, quarterly invoicing (as opposed to monthly), management reports, price stability for a fixed period, free delivery or increased delivery frequency. Remember, the supplier wants to maintain your business and may be able to help in other ways.

Action checklist – General hints/good practice

1. Establish a code of ethics

- Respect confidentiality – do not disclose suppliers' prices and methods of trading to competitors.
- Declare any personal interest.
- Do not accept gifts from suppliers or potential suppliers (it is good practice to advise all suppliers of this in writing when you commence trading with them and prior to the Christmas period when most suppliers traditionally bear gifts!).

2. Beware

- If you have a roll-over contract, make sure you know when you have to give notice should you wish to terminate.
- Be aware of authority limits and do not exceed your authority.
- Never make assumptions – ensure all details are clarified in writing.

3. Fulfil your side of the contract

Ensure payment is made in accord with your agreement.

4. Maintain an audit trail

Always maintain an audit trail of all purchase documents.

Dos and don'ts for effective purchasing

Do

- Involve your internal customers in the purchasing process.
- Assess and visit your suppliers regularly.
- Build relationships with suppliers based upon mutual trust and good communication.
- Establish a clear code of ethics.

Don't

- Allow yourself to be dragged into a 'Dutch auction' by your suppliers.
- Stay with the same supplier 'because you've always used them' – be sure you're using them 'because they're the best'.

Useful reading

Managing purchasing: sourcing and contracting, Andrew Erridge, Oxford: Butterworth-Heinemann, 1995

Successful purchasing in a week, 2nd ed, Stephen Carter, London: Hodder & Stoughton, 1998

Buying business equipment and services: a management guide, Kingston upon Thames: Croner Publications, 1995, Amendment service available by annual subscription.

Are you managing purchasing: a guide to better buying, Malcolm Jones, London: Nicholas Brealey Publishing, 1992

Purchasing: principles and applications, 7th ed, Stuart F Heinritz, Paul V Farrell and Clifton L Smith, Englewood Cliffs, NJ: Prentice-Hall, 1986

Useful address

Chartered Institute of Purchasing and Supply, Easton House, Easton on the Hill, Stamford, Lincolnshire PE9 3NZ, Tel: 01780 56777

Thought starters

- How much do you know about your organisation's annual purchases?
- What is your organisation's annual spend with each of its major suppliers?
- How often have you visited your major suppliers?

Drawing Up a Contract of Employment

This checklist details the steps involved in drawing up a contract of employment. It is primarily aimed at new contracts, but many points will also be useful to those who have to modify an existing contract. As with any legal document it is essential that advice is sought before a contract is put into effect.

Legislation does not require that an organisation has to have a formal written contract with its employees, but such a contract can prevent disputes over terms and conditions at a later date, whereas oral agreements can often be called into question.

MCI Standards

This checklist has relevance for the MCI Management Standards: Key Role C – Manage People.

Definition

A contract of employment is a legally enforceable agreement, either oral or written, between an employer and employee that defines terms and conditions to which both parties must adhere. Areas covered include job title, remuneration, holidays, sick pay, location, mobility, and the period of employment. Extra clauses can be added which restrain the employee after termination of employment, or make a certain qualification or confidentiality a prerequisite of the job.

Advantages of contracts of employment

Having well-drafted contracts of employment means that:

- employees can be clear about their rights
- costs incurred by disputes over terms and conditions can be avoided
- the employer can justifiably terminate employment if an employee does not meet the contract's requirements.

Disadvantages of contracts of employment

There are no real disadvantages to contracts of employment. Writing one that is water-tight but allows both parties some flexibility is difficult. Contracts require resources to draw up and review, and if they are badly written they can do the organisation more harm than good.

Action checklist

1. Analyse the job to be contracted

Look at the job description if there is one, as this will provide information on what the employee's job entails. Clauses in the contract must allow the employee to carry out their duties without restrictions. The post may require the person to have a professional qualification – would the person be allowed to continue in the role if the awarding body were to withdraw their professional status?

2. Consider future plans and objectives

Would you expect the size of the workforce to be reduced in the future? If so, a permanent contract may not be appropriate. A particular job title may not be suitable if you have to transfer the employee to a different department; a general title, such as 'Admin Officer' may offer more scope for change. If you have plans to open further sites throughout the country, you may need to incorporate a mobility clause to cater for employees who will have to work there from time to time. By including clauses such as mobility, the organisation can ensure that its workforce will adapt to its future needs and developments.

3. Look back at problems

The organisation may have had problems with contracts of employment in the past. This could have been due to the nature of the work the organisation does, for example, or an employee could have left taking some customers with them in the process, or have created some intellectual property whose ownership is disputed, or have resisted relocation because a contractual statement was lacking.

4. Gather information and confer with colleagues

Try to obtain some sample contracts of employment used in organisations in the same field, and get hold of literature relating to the current requirements of personnel legislation. Colleagues can offer good advice over what has and has not worked in the past, both in the current organisation and others in which they may have worked. Trade union representatives can point out contentious issues that may arise.

If your organisation has a legal department, consult it. If not, be prepared to go outside; costs incurred here could well save in the long term.

5. Incorporate written particulars

The Employment Protection (Consolidation) Act (EPCA) 1978 and the Trade Union Reform and Employment Rights Act (TURERA) 1993 require that all employees whose employment lasts over a month, irrespective of the number of hours they work, are given a written statement of employment particulars. The Acts do not make it necessary to include these particulars in a contract of employment but it is advisable that they are, so that the employee has one document which contains all matters relating to their relationship with the employer.

The particulars that must be given to the employee are:

- the employer's and employee's names
- the date the employment started and will end (if fixed term), or the period it is expected to last if temporary
- the rate of remuneration or how it is calculated, and when it is paid
- terms and conditions relating to hours of work, holidays, holiday pay, sickness and sick pay, and pensions and pension schemes
- the notice required to be given by both employee and employer to terminate employment
- any collective agreements which affect the terms and conditions of employment, for example, those negotiated by a trade union (even if the employee is not a member)
- the job title
- disciplinary rules (or reference to a set of disciplinary rules), the person to whom an employee can apply and the manner in which the application is to be made if the employee is not satisfied with a decision concerning a matter of discipline. The legislation requires this only for organisations with over 20 employees.
- the name of the person who can be approached and the procedure to follow regarding any grievance related to employment
- details of the place(s) of work
- the length of time and currency in which remuneration will be made if the employee is required to work abroad for a period of more than one month.

These written particulars must be given to employees within two months of commencement of employment.

In cases where another document can be referred to, such as a disciplinary procedure, a staff handbook can be used. This document must be accessible; a copy should be given to the employee as part of their induction.

6. Consider possible extra clauses

There are a number of clauses that may be included in a contract of employment, depending on the nature of the job and the needs of the organisation.

Relocation expenses – it may be appropriate to include a clause which requires an employee to repay any relocation expenses incurred if they leave within a certain period.

Uniform or clothing – where there is a standard dress code or protective clothing is needed, make this clear in the contract. Check on sex discrimination legislation over differences between male and female appearance.

Qualifications – if the jobholder is required to obtain or hold a certain qualification by a certain date (educational or professional), define which one and the consequences of failing to have it. Where the employee is funded to obtain a qualification, they may be required to repay the cost if they terminate their employment within a certain period.

Driving licence – employment may be terminated if the employee loses their licence.

Mobility – where the employee is expected to work at different bases, make it clear.

Travel – for many jobs it is necessary to travel to meet customers or clients, so you may need to include a clause to cover this. Clerical workers are usually only expected to be as mobile as far as is reasonably possible on a daily commuting basis, whereas managers can be expected to travel as far as the business requires.

Probation – if a probationary period is used for new employees then its length should be given, with the ability to terminate the contract at the end or an earlier date, or to extend the length of the probation. Include a statement which says that permanent employment will be confirmed in writing, subject to the probationary period being completed satisfactorily.

Retirement – it should be made clear that the contract is terminated when the employee reaches the organisation's set retirement age.

Restraints – it is possible in some circumstances to restrain the activities of an employee once employment has terminated. Examples include the use of trade secrets that the individual acquired while working for an organisation, or working for another organisation in the same trade and geographical area. Expert advice is essential here as the law is a minefield in this area; the employer must show that the restraining clauses are no more than what is required to protect their interests.

Drawing Up a Contract of Employment

7. Produce a draft

Have it checked over, preferably by someone with legal expertise. Ensure that all terms are clear and unambiguous, and do not restrict the employee from carrying out or further developing the role.

8. Review the contract

The employee should be made aware that signing the contract is tantamount to a legally binding contract and therefore subject to the law of the land.

Although the employee should not have signed the contract if they are not happy with it, ask them, at a later date, if there is something that they think needs changing. Remember that you can't make any changes to the contract without the employee's consent. Problems that occur elsewhere in the organisation may affect contracts wholesale, so be aware. Keep an eye on the personnel literature for court cases and changes in legislation which may affect current or future contracts.

Dos and don'ts for drawing up a contract of employment

Do
- Take time to prepare by examining the job and the future of the role.
- Get an idea of the law relating to contracts of employment.
- Use clear and unambiguous wording in the contract.

Don't
- Forget to draw on the experiences of your colleagues.
- Cut corners – pay for legal advice if it is not available internally.
- Try to restrain the employee too much – allow for some flexibility in the contract.

Useful reading

BOOKS

Contracts and terms and conditions of employment, Peter Burgess (ed), London: Institute of Personnel and Development, 1995

Tolley's drafting contracts of employment, Gillian Howard, Croydon: Tolley, 1993

JOURNAL ARTICLES

Contracts of employment and implied terms 1. IDS Brief, No 562, April 1996, pp7–10

Particulars of employment, Sarah de Gay, Tolley's Employment Law and Practice, Vol 1 no 4, October 1995, pp29–30

Restraining influences, Olga Aikin, Personnel Management, Vol 26 no 6, June 1994, pp65–66

How to draft an employment contract, Alan Fowler, Personnel Management Plus, Vol 4 no 12, December 1993, pp23–24

Thought starters

- Do you know what is in your contract of employment?
- Have you ever had a problem with your contract of employment? What was it?
- Do you know of any case where a contract of employment has been called into question? What happened?
- Has anyone left your organisation and taken staff/customers with them? Could they have been prevented from doing so?

Preparing and Using Job Descriptions

This checklist provides guidance for those wishing to write a job description for a new post or to update an existing one.

Drawing up job descriptions for a department helps to ensure that work is organised into jobs that occupy a person full time, and to check that each job is justified. Job descriptions provide the basis for the preparation of key results and objectives for the organisation, each function and each person in it, making sure that these fit into a coherent whole. A job description can help a candidate to gain a picture of what the job is about, and can provide the recruiter with a checklist of requirements against which to match candidates. Once in post, an employee will have a list of main responsibilities and important contacts through direct working relationships. The organisation will find job descriptions essential in job evaluation and assessments; they are also helpful when settling disputes about duties, whilst permitting some flexibility.

MCI Standards

This checklist has relevance for the MCI Management Standards: Key Role C – Manage People.

Definition

A job description is a structured and factual statement of a job's function and objectives, the acceptable standards of performance and the boundaries of the job holder's authority. The job title, department, location, and to and for whom the job holder is responsible, are also included.

Advantages of job descriptions

Job descriptions:

- are useful in the recruitment process
- are an aid in planning objectives and obtaining training requirements
- are essential for clarifying boundaries of responsibility and decision making.

Disadvantages of job descriptions

They:

- can create a 'that's not in my job description!' environment if too restrictive
- need regular updating.

Action checklist

1. Inform staff of the reasons for reviewing and amending job descriptions

When existing job descriptions are reviewed, it is important to inform employees what is happening and why, to guard against employees feeling threatened. A statement should be made to the effect that the exercise will be carried out, with the full involvement of the job holders, with the objectives being, for example:

- to identify all interdepartmental working links
- to help plan objectives and training programmes
- to ensure that functions have the correct number of staff for their workload
- to give everyone a clear understanding of how the company is organised.

2. Assign responsibility

In some cases job descriptions are prepared by personnel departments and agreed with the job holder and manager, but this is generally undesirable. The exercise should be done by the job holder and manager with guidance about form and content available from the personnel department.

A central function, usually the personnel department, should be assigned to check job descriptions for consistency and overlap. In doing this the following points should be considered:

- Does each job holder have a clear line of authority?
- Does each job holder report to the right person?
- Do too many employees report directly to one manager, who may be unable to cope with their supervision properly?
- Are there too many levels of authority?
- Are some jobs so similar as to be essentially the same?
- Are staff and line functions clearly defined?
- Are similar functions grouped together or are there odd jobs in unrelated departments which clearly belong elsewhere?
- Are specific tasks and objectives passed down from the centre which can be followed downwards through individual job descriptions?

- Are there any 'gaps', ie jobs for which no one has been assigned responsibility?

3. Gather information

The person responsible for compiling the job description should consider:

- what management wants from the job
- what the job holder thinks he or she is doing and what he or she is actually doing
- what others, whose work interacts with the job holder, think he or she is doing and ought to be doing.

This information should be gained from informal interviews. If resources are limited, it is possible to use questionnaires, but the results tend to be ambiguous, and the time required to analyse the completed questionnaires can exceed the interviewing time. Employees can be asked to complete a diary over a short period of time, but generally employees dislike this, and it should be avoided.

4. Put together the job description

The job description should contain:

a) Basic information

Job title and department – the job title should be readily understood inside and outside the organisation. Remember that other employees will consider the status of those with the same kind of job title to be equal. Do not use over-elaborate job titles.

Location – the location of the job should be given. If some flexibility is expected then it is wise not to define the location too tightly, but to state that the normal location may change from time to time.

Responsibility to – the names of the people who are responsible for supervision, discipline, etc.

Responsibility for – include the total number of staff for whom they are responsible, with the names of those reporting directly to the job holder. For example, 'responsible for 30 staff through 3 supervisors'.

Major functional relationships – an organisation chart will show how a job fits into the organisation and its relationship with other jobs. For example, a works personnel officer may report directly to the works manager but a dotted line should also show the personnel officer reporting to the company personnel manager.

b) Principal purpose or objective of the job

This should be a short statement describing why the job exists. For example, for a sales manager it could be simply 'ensuring that sales targets are achieved'.

c) Main duties/key tasks/key result areas

Key tasks, or responsibilities, are those which make a substantial contribution towards the job objectives and those of the organisation. These form the main part of the job description and there should be no more than eight to ten tasks listed, rather than a list of all the job holder's tasks. To ensure against too restrictive a job description, an open-ended statement should be included. A standard statement is: 'Such duties as are considered essential for effective operations and services'. This should form the final key task. Distinguish between those tasks which are the direct responsibility of the job holder and those which he or she delegates to others to carry out.

The job description should allow for an individual to use his or her initiative, and where results are measurable in some way, these should be stated. Results expected should be concrete, specific, attainable and worthwhile. Where levels of achievement are specified in measurements, it is particularly important that these are regularly updated.

Once the key tasks have been identified they should be put into some sort of order, which might be chronological, by relative importance, by frequency of performance, by similar sorts of tasks, or by all tasks related to a particular aspect of the job. Each task should be described in a sentence or two which explains what is done, how and why. Sentences should begin with action verbs, with imprecise phrases like 'responsible for' avoided.

5. Update and review

The job description must be kept up-to-date and should be examined at least:

- once a year when the job holder is appraised
- when a job falls vacant, to ensure that the description still meets the department's requirements
- after the new job holder has been in post a few months to take account of any significant changes in the job holder's duties.

Dos and don'ts for preparing a job description

Do

- Involve the current job holder.
- Check job descriptions in 'surrounding' areas of work to ensure a close fit and no clashes.
- Make updating job descriptions a regular process.

Don't

- Forget to let staff know why job descriptions are being amended or updated.
- Restrict the employee's initiative through the job description.

Useful reading

Books

How to write a job description, Bernard Ungerson, London: Institute of Personnel Management, 1983

A guide to writing job descriptions, International Computers Limited Remuneration Planning Department, London: International Computers Limited

Journal articles

The importance of the job description, Frank Walton, Employment Bulletin and Industrial Relations Digest, Vol 5 no 2, February 1989, pp5–7

Writing job descriptions that get results, Roger J Plachy, Personnel, October 1987, pp56–63

Thought starters

- Do you know what's in your job description?
- Would you change your job description in any way?
- Is your job description up-to-date?

Marketing for the Small Business

This checklist is designed to help you to identify those goods and services that customers will buy and how you can best promote them in order to make your business a success.

Some aspects of marketing are indispensable to a small firm if it is to survive and prosper. Too many owners of small firms see the choice as no marketing effort at all on the one hand or trying to emulate Unilever or Esso on the other. There are many steps in between from which the successful small business owner may benefit.

MCI Standards

This checklist has relevance for the MCI Management Standards: Key Role A – Manage Activities.

Definition

Successful marketing will ensure that you produce the right goods and services, at the right price, for the right people, at the right time, and in the right place.

Marketing involves the identification and profitable satisfaction of customers' needs. The customer exchanges one 'good' (usually money) for another (usually products or services). Marketing is concerned with studying the attitudes and needs of different categories of customer, identifying customer needs that the business can satisfy, and satisfying those needs, at a profit, in the most cost-effective way.

Promotion, or sales promotion as it is often known, is part of marketing and involves the use of advertising, the offer of incentives, publicity and personal selling. Selling and marketing are not the same thing. Selling is the final step in the marketing process.

For the small business, marketing in its broadest sense may seem expensive and time-consuming. If you allow it to be expensive it will be. Ineffective marketing will target the wrong people and convey incorrect messages about you, your products and your services.

Action checklist

1. Subject your business to a SWOT analysis

SWOT analysis requires you to identify the internal Strengths and
Weaknesses of your business and the external Opportunities for and Threats
to it in the business environment. You need to identify all the relevant
factors affecting your business and to list them under the four SWOT
categories. Examples of SWOT factors follow.

Strengths

- The unique selling point (USP) that differentiates your products and
  services from those of your competitors.
- Higher skill levels that provide you with an advantage over your competitors.
- Your awareness of the market and potential opportunities.
- A well-developed business network that ensures that you and your products
  are well-known.
- Effective cost control and highly competitive pricing.
- Well-trained staff.

Weaknesses

- Inadequate working capital.
- Inadequate managerial skills.
- Poorly trained staff.
- Insufficient space for expansion to meet demand.
- Lack of new product development to meet customer demand.
- Ineffective marketing and promotion.
- Out-of-date plant and equipment.

Opportunities

- Changing tastes of customers in favour of items which are, or could be,
  strongly represented in your product range.
- New legislation generating an increasing need for your goods/services.
- The arrival of a large business in the area which may require goods/services
  like those you supply.
- Closure of a competitor's business.

Threats

- Price competition, which usually takes the form of lower prices or discounts offered by your competitors.
- Increased prices for raw or finished materials or for services which you
  buy in.
- Legislation imposing new obligations or restrictions.
- Poor performance by the national economy, high interest rates or
  depressed consumer spending.

These are all threats likely to have a more immediate impact on small firms than on bigger firms with more resources and reserves, and with more opportunity to diversify. Consider whether you can turn any of your weaknesses into strengths, or threats into opportunities.

2. Analyse the goods and services provided by your firm

- How much do you depend upon suppliers and related businesses?
- Can your suppliers influence the way you do business?
- Are your services and products in a growth sector?
- Will future demand increase, remain stable or decrease?
- What is the nature of the competition – what do your competitors supply?
- How are your services or products similar to, or different from, those of your competitors?
- Can demand be generated by promotion?
- What action can you take to change the situation to the advantage of your business?

3. Look at market segmentation

You need to consider carefully:

- the limits of the geographical area of your activities – the further you go from base the more it may cost you to deliver and the less profit you may make
- the product mix which you intend to offer, as this can be crucial to your profitability – too high a percentage of your turnover allocated to products or services with low or negative margins could spell disaster
- which people or companies are your targets or customers – some customers want cheap goods and services; some will regard cheapness as a sign of poor quality. You can't please everyone; you must decide whom you are aiming to please.
- the products and services you intend to offer – a decision which will depend on your choice of potential customers. It is essential to keep products under regular review. All products have a life-cycle, after which sales and revenue will tend to decline.

4. Identify your product

Think in terms of the specialist skills, knowledge and capability that you have, or what you could do to improve existing market products. Can you offer an obviously superior product for the same or slightly more money?

5. Identify and set the right price for your goods and services

You will not necessarily wish to gain a reputation for the highest prices in the marketplace. Nor may you wish to be regarded as a 'price-cutter'. You need to recover your costs and to make a satisfactory margin over and above these. Consider:

- your competitors' prices for similar products and services
- the possibility of offering differential prices to selected customers
- individual costs – including overheads – for each of your products or services
- whether to actively promote loss-making products or services
- customer perception of the value of your products/services in meeting their needs. Will customers pay more for yours because they meet their needs better?

6. Identify the most appropriate location for your business

How important is location in marketing and sales promotion for your business? Are visibility and accessibility important?

- Do your customers come to see you or do you go to them?
- How do your customers usually contact you – face to face, on the telephone, by fax or email?
- Do you need a 'shopfront'?
- Do you need to be physically near to your customers?
- Will public transport systems and access routes be important?
- Could you work effectively from home?

7. Consider and carry out an appropriate level of market research

You need to know as much as possible about your competitors' activities. Be sure that rumour and fact are not confused. Sources of useful information include government statistics, trade directories, national and local newspapers, and the trade press (your public library may be able to help). Try your local Business Link and Chamber of Commerce as well.

8. Carry out the marketing and monitor the results

The result of your research will lead you to carry out a marketing campaign to a certain set of potential customers. This will involve advertising, publicity, press announcements, perhaps setting up a website on the Internet, perhaps some direct mail to specific customers, or a scattergun approach to see how many people may be interested.

The design of promotional literature and the exploitation of marketing techniques can require guidance and advice. Consultants may prove too expensive but do seek advice from your local Business Link, TEC, Chamber of Commerce or Business Club, or nearest regional office of the DTI.

Whatever you do – and however you do it – do be prepared for customer reaction – and demand – even if it is minimal. And do try to monitor where most interest comes from so that you can target better next time.

Dos and don'ts for marketing for the small business

Do
- Base your decisions on accurate information about your costs.
- Keep a careful eye on your product mix.
- Talk regularly to your bank manager.

Don't
- Fall into the trap of trying to compete on price alone.
- Take decisions except in the context of a planned strategy.
- Assume that, because profit requires sales, sales equal profit.

Useful reading

Successful marketing for a small business, 3rd ed, Dave Patten, London: Kogan Page, 1995

Successful marketing in a week, 2nd ed, E Davies and B J Davies, London: Hodder & Stoughton, 1998

How to do your own advertising, 2nd ed, Michael Bennie, Plymouth: How To Books, 1996

Successful market research in a week, Matthew Housden, London: Hodder & Stoughton, 1992

Thought starters

- Why should anybody buy what you are offering?
- Are you sure that you have identified your competitors?
- What distinguishes you from your competitors?
- What picture do you think people in your town have of you and your business?
- How can you brighten up your image?
- Can the local press help you?

Preparing a Marketing Plan

This checklist focuses on the standard model of marketing planning endorsed by several writers in the field. The model contains formalised procedures, although the degree to which these are followed will depend on the culture and requirements of the organisation.

The discipline of marketing planning has been widely debated. Depending on their standpoint, academics have defended the standard textbook model or proposed alternative versions. McDonald, one of the principal writers in the field, in his article **Ten barriers to marketing planning**, acknowledges that 'marketing planning is still the most enigmatic of all the problems facing management.'

MCI standards

This checklist has relevance for the MCI Management Standards: Key Role A – Manage Activities.

Definition

'Marketing planning is simply a logical sequence and a series of activities leading to the setting of marketing objectives and the formulation of plans for achieving them.' McDonald, as above.

Advantages of formalised procedures

- They encourage a rational approach to making business decisions.
- Everyone follows the same strategy thus reducing potential conflicts, misunderstandings and operational difficulties.
- They allow senior management to set out marketing strategy while leaving the day-to-day implementation to junior management.
- They help to highlight areas you might otherwise miss.

Disadvantages of formalised procedures

- They form a complex process which needs basic knowledge and skills.
- They are time consuming and therefore costly to construct and follow.
- There is a loss of flexibility for firms composed of small business units.
- They can tend to take over and become an end in themselves.

Action checklist

1. Set strategic objectives

These have been traditionally set by top management although current practice is to employ more democratic processes involving the key stakeholders if not all the staff. They are not usually within the brief of the market planner alone. They must be kept firmly in mind and the strategies and action plans drawn up must be broadly in line with them. The market planning process can't go forward without them. The written plan should include a copy of the strategic objectives and the organisation's mission statement.

2. Carry out a marketing audit

This process enables a company to analyse and understand the environment in which it operates. It is the key to the SWOT analysis, the next stage in the marketing planning process. It is carried out in two parts: the external audit and the internal audit. The external audit should cover the business and economic environment, the market and the competition; this should examine the important trends which have affected and which will be affecting the market and the industry. It also involves searching questions about competitors and customers, now and in the future. The internal audit should concentrate on the planner's own company, its operational efficiency and service effectiveness, its key skills, competences and resources, its products / services and the 'core' business it is in.

3. Carry out a SWOT analysis

This is a summary of the audit under the headings Strengths, Weaknesses, Opportunities and Threats and should be included in the final written plan. Strengths and weaknesses refer to the company and its internal environment while opportunities and threats are external factors over which the company has no control but which it must anticipate, evaluate and try to exploit. Only key data should be included. See Performing a SWOT Analysis on page 121 for further information.

4. Make assumptions

These assumptions are the strategic drivers of the marketing plan and they may relate to economic, technological or competitive factors. Assumptions should be based on accurate information and sensible estimates of what can be achieved in the light of past performance. Sound information is problematic because the pace of change is making the future discontinuous from the past. Coming up with viable and challenging assumptions involves creative, lateral thinking and breaking with the past. Only a few major assumptions should be included in the written plan.

5. Set marketing objectives

This is the central step in the marketing planning process because the setting of achievable and realistic objectives is based on the analysis of the marketing audit, while strategy decisions cannot be made without reference to objectives. Marketing objectives are concerned with which products are to be sold in which markets: it is important not to confuse objectives (what you want to do) with strategies (how you are going to do it). The objectives should be included in the written plan.

6. Estimate expected results

Marketing objectives should be SMART: Specific, Measurable, Achievable, Realistic and Time-tabled. For example, *'to gain a 6% share of the overall market'* or *'to achieve 600 customers by the end of the year'*. Terms such as *'increase'* or *'maximise'* should not be used unless they can be quantified.

7. Generate marketing strategies

These are the broad methods by which the marketing objectives will be achieved and they describe the means of doing so within the required time. They are generally referred to as the marketing mix or as the four Ps: Product – what are its benefits to the customer; Price – how it is priced to attract the right, or the appropriate customer base; Place – who are those customers; Promotion – how may they be reached. They should appear in the written plan.

8. Define programmes

The general strategies must be developed so that they have their own programmes or action plans. The combination of these plans and their relative importance will depend on the company. A large company with several different functions or departments may have several plans covering advertising, sales promotion, pricing and so on. Other companies may have one plan, for example, a product plan embracing all four Ps. Details of the programmes should be included in the written plan.

9. Communicate the plan

Everyone should understand the plan. It is advisable to make a presentation of it rather than to circulate written copies. If the plan is not effectively communicated, it will fail.

10. Measure and review progress

The plan should be monitored as it progresses. Make sure the measures you collect are meaningful to the success of the plan. If circumstances change, it should be revised to take advantage of unforeseen opportunities or to counter unforeseen threats. Details of how this should be done need to be included in the written plan and should relate directly to stages 4–9 above.

Dos and don'ts for marketing planning

Do

- Be clear on the organisation's strategic objectives.
- Adjust the plan to suit the size, culture and circumstances of the organisation.
- Consult on and communicate the plan.
- Be aware that it is a time-consuming exercise.

Don't

- Confuse objectives (what you want to achieve) with strategies (how you are trying to achieve them).
- Neglect to analyse information carefully and spend too long on projecting future markets from historical data.
- Forget the plan is a means to achieve objectives, not a rigid control mechanism.
- Let the planners alter the shape of the objectives.

Useful reading

Books

Successful marketing plans in a week, 2nd ed, Ros Jay, London: Hodder & Stoughton, 1998

Marketing plans: how to prepare them how to use them, 3rd ed, Malcolm H B McDonald, Oxford: Heinemann Professional, 1995

The marketing plan: a practitioner's guide, John Westwood, London: Kogan Page, 1990

The 12 day marketing plan: construct a marketing programme that really works in less than two weeks, James C Makens, Wellingborough: Thorsons, 1989

Journal articles

Ten barriers to marketing planning, Malcolm H B McDonald, Journal of Marketing Management, vol 5 no 1, Summer 1989, pp1–18

Marketing plans or marketing planning? Laura Cousins, Business Strategy Review, Vol 2 no 2, Summer 1991, pp35–54

Marketing planning: observations on current practices and recent studies, Tom Griffin, European Journal of Marketing, Vol 23 no 12, 1989, pp21–35

Useful addresses

Chartered Institute of Marketing, Moor Hall, Cookham, Maidenhead, Berkshire SL6 9QH, Tel: 01628 427500

The Institute of Management, Cottingham Road, Corby, Northants NN17 1TT, Tel: 01536 204222

Institute of Sales and Marketing Management, 31 Upper George Street, Luton LU1 2RD, Tel: 01582 411130

Marketing Society, 206 Worple Road, London SW20 8PN, Tel: 0181 879 3464

Thought starters

- Is your marketing unsystematic, opportunistic, haphazard or initiative-led?
- Have you set measurable market targets in the past?
- Are your marketing objectives and tactics known and coordinated throughout the organisation?
- Do you really know what your customers think of you?
- Is your market stable, and your market position secure?

Carrying Out Marketing Research

> This checklist has been designed to explain the basic steps of marketing research.
>
> The use of marketing research has become increasingly prevalent since the 1980s. This has partly happened as a result of the quality revolution that swept through many organisations. At the heart of the quality movement is the notion that organisations need to get close to customers; in order to get close to customers, they need to listen to what those customers really want. Marketing research is one of the main ways of finding this out.

MCI Standards

This checklist has relevance for the MCI Management Standards: Key Roles A and D – Manage Activities and Manage Information.

Definition

For the purposes of this checklist, market research and marketing research are interchangeable terms, that are used to define a data gathering and analysis process which aims to provide information on the sale of products or services, and the customers who buy them.

But the research process goes a lot further into the areas of:

- market size and key market sectors
- market brand shares
- identifying potential customers
- identifying needs that may not have been articulated
- information on competitors
- defining actual and potential market sizes.

While there is much that marketing research can do, mostly it is directed towards discovering which groups or market sectors will buy your product, and what improvements, replacements or new related products may be desirable.

There is a range of different methodologies for carrying out marketing research – surveys, questionnaires, High Street or door-to-door interviews or discussion groups.

Advantages of carrying out marketing research

Effective marketing research can help organisations to:

- direct their energies towards the real needs of customers
- avoid wasting money on developing a product customers don't want
- develop a real customer focus and keep in touch with customers – the information gathered by marketing research is vital for developing the organisation's corporate strategy
- obtain a snapshot of what customers, or potential customers, feel and think at any particular time.

Issues to remember when carrying out marketing research

- If you don't define clearly what you want to find out, then the results you get back are likely to be unhelpful.
- What you get back will be the results of research, not necessarily reliable intelligence, with no guarantee of accuracy.
- Marketing research can be time-consuming and expensive.

Action checklist

1. Be clear about the purpose of the marketing research

How will you use the results? For instance to:

- develop performance indicators?
- develop standards?
- develop new products or services?
- discontinue or adapt product lines?
- improve quality?
- increase market share?

2. Decide what you want to find out

All too often marketing research fails because people aren't clear exactly what they want to find out. Hold a brainstorming meeting with the key people within your organisation to establish objectives for the research. A golden rule is that you should not try to cover too much in one exercise.

3. Be clear about who your customers are

The key stage of any marketing research is to decide whom it is you want to question. List all the types of customers you either have at the moment, or would like to appeal to, and target these people with your marketing research. Desk research – ie pulling together all the existing information you can find to help make some preliminary deductions – can be really helpful here.

4. Develop a brief

The brief is a clear statement of what is expected, by when and at what price. The brief will require you to:

- be specific on the particular market objectives at which the research is aimed
- describe any background information that can make a significant contribution
- suggest ideas on methods to be explored
- specify deadlines for delivery
- indicate requirements on confidentiality, disclosure and presentation
- indicate a date to take the brief forward (with shortlisted candidates if appointing an external agency).

If the research is to be done in-house, the brief is a key document. If you are going to select an external agency, it becomes essential.

5. Decide who's going to carry out the marketing research

If your organisation does not have a marketing research department (or sometimes, even if it does), you may need to bring in a specialist organisation to help you. If you feel you need to call in outside help, ask the following questions:

- What budget do you have? How much expert advice can you afford?
- How much time can you devote to the research?
- How much expertise do you have? Marketing research is a science as well as a skilled art.
- Do you have the resources? These include computer processing capability and statistical expertise as well as research experience.

6. Select an external agency

Find the names of suitable agencies through the trade press or trade association, directories, or contacts and recommendations. Establish some selection criteria, in addition to price, appearance and promise, such as reputation, membership of a professional body, track record, customer list, and any conflict of interests. Circulate your brief and shortlist candidates from their responses.

7. Choose your method

There are two main types of research, each of which has its own individual methods.

Qualitative research usually involves smaller groups than quantitative research. This is particularly useful when you are dealing with sensitive issues. In qualitative research, the questions are usually open, and concentrate on feelings. Qualitative research is not good for considering trends over a wide section of the community; it is better at helping you to flesh out the main issues.

In many ways, people see qualitative research as an effective way of getting insight into the way people feel and think. There are a number of methods involved in qualitative research. These include face-to-face interviews, taped interviews, telephone interviews, postal surveys and group discussions.

You may want to use more than one method: postal surveys, for example, can deal with large numbers superficially, while group discussions deal with small numbers in depth. There is often an inverse relationship between validity (whether you are measuring exactly what you want to measure) and reliability (whether the results are likely to be reproducible).

Quantitative research works mainly through the use of surveys carried out with a carefully selected sample of people and asks closed questions requiring specific answers such as:

- how much would you be prepared to pay?
- how satisfied were you?
- do you prefer this in blue, red or pink?

Quantitative research is useful because you can start putting percentage figures to your findings. In other words, if you ask a hundred people the same closed question, you can find out the percentage either agreeing or disagreeing.

8. Think about data analysis

As you put your research instrument together, think how you are going to store, sort and analyse the data contained in the returns. Think about ease of data entry, how any statistical or decision support package will manipulate the data, and how not to become a slave to a particular technique. Your results will need interpretation and understanding even if sophisticated techniques have been used. Remember that there are lies, damned lies and then there are statistics. Be wary of making sweeping assumptions from low returns but do look for the significant differences and relationships.

Marketing research sometimes throws up unexpected findings that shed new light on the issue. Be alert to the possibility of such findings when looking at the data and cross-analyses you want to perform.

Dos and don'ts for carrying out marketing research

Do

- Take time to plan research.
- Decide which kind of research is appropriate for you.
- Be clear about what you want to find out.
- Be prepared for surprises.

Don't

- Rush to start the research or jump to conclusions with the results.
- Ignore the results.
- Think marketing research is something you only do once – it should be ongoing.

Useful reading

Using market research to grow your business: how management obtain the information they need, Robin J Birn, London: Pitman, 1994

Successful market research in a week, Matthew Housden, London: Hodder & Stoughton, 1992

Understanding and designing market research, John R Webb, London: Academic Press, 1992

A handbook of market research techniques, Robin Birn, Paul Hague and Phyllis Vangelder, New York: Prentice Hall, 1990

Useful addresses

Chartered Institute of Marketing, Moor Hall, Cookham, Maidenhead, Berkshire SL6 9QH, Tel: 01628 427500

Market Research Society, 15 Northburgh Street, London EC1V 0AH, Tel: 0171 490 4911

Thought starters

- How well do you really know what your customers want?
- Do you really need to carry out marketing research?
- Which method is most appropriate to you – qualitative or quantitative research?
- Have you got a good source of advice for finding out which type of marketing research would suit your purposes?

Successful Direct Mail

This checklist provides guidance for those who wish to undertake a direct mail advertising campaign.

Information technology has allowed such campaigns to become increasingly sophisticated as an enormous amount of information can be collected, stored and retrieved on both industrial and private consumers. It is now possible to obtain highly specific lists of addresses on particular groups to which an organisation or individual can send direct mail to advertise their products or services. Companies are collecting information on their customers, ranging from their birthdays to their purchasing habits, so they can tailor a marketing message particular to each individual.

This one-to-one form of communication can be very effective, but to do it properly requires careful planning and designing. The scale of the direct mail campaign and the number of customers contacted will depend on the size of the organisation (ranging from single individuals to multi-national corporations) and the resources available; the procedure, however, remains the same.

MCI Standards

This checklist has relevance for the MCI Management Standards: Key Roles A and B – Manage Activities and Manage Resources.

Definition

Direct mail is a method of advertising a product or service using letters, cards or leaflets sent through the post and personally addressed to a selected list of individuals or organisations.

Advantages of direct mail

- Individuals are communicated with on a person-to-person level.
- Wastage is low as targeted individuals are carefully selected.
- Effectiveness is easily and quickly measured.
- Initial testing is easy (by sending out to a sample of addresses).

Disadvantages of direct mail

- People are often wary of/uninterested in unsolicited ('junk') mail – many hate it.
- A suitable mailing list must be available – it can be expensive to research and build up a suitable list.
- An up-to-date and accurate mailing list is a relative rarity.

Action checklist

1. Define the terms of reference

Identify what you want to achieve by using direct mail. Is it, for example, a general awareness campaign or is it to help launch a new service or product? The target audience for the campaign should be defined. Are there sectors who do not use the service or product, or are there those who subscribe in larger quantities? Identify the profile of your best customers and you will identify the profile of your best prospects. Assign a budget for the campaign.

2. Decide who is to run the campaign

Appoint an agency to run the campaign. This may be your own marketing department if you have one which is large enough, or a special working party drawn from your organisation. Consider contracting the work out to an external consultant if you feel you lack the necessary expertise internally. This may prove to be more expensive, but a badly run campaign is not just ineffective, it can also be damaging to an organisation's reputation.

3. Prepare or obtain a mailing list

Evaluate the usefulness of the information on in-house databases. If there are limitations suggest improvements, or if an in-house database doesn't exist, consider the benefits and costs of starting one.

It will be much cheaper to purchase a mailing list from a specialist company. Make sure you check the company's reputation for producing lists. The addressee information must be up-to-date and accurate. Nobody likes receiving mail with their name misspelled or seeing the addressee as someone who moved 4 years ago, or two copies addressed to slightly different people. It is also a waste of money sending mail to someone for whom the product or service is totally irrelevant.

4. Design the mailing

Check out in-house capability of designing advertising material. Be creative when designing the mailing (including the envelope) to attract and hold the attention of the addressee. Make it look as personal as possible – many people bin computer-addressed envelopes on sight. Ensure that the design matches the type of target; for example, the style appropriate for teenagers will differ from that appropriate to senior managers. Consider contracting out the design stage to an appropriate agency if your organisation lacks expertise. Remember: it is more effective to mail a smaller number of professional looking documents that have incurred the additional expense of a design agency than a large number of cheaper, poorly designed in-house ones.

Where the addressee needs to get back in touch offer a stimulus for an early response, possibly a discount or free gift, as the longer a person leaves mail unanswered the less likely they are to bother. In cases which need a mailed response enclose a postage-paid envelope and don't ask for too much information; minimise the time and complexity involved to complete the form. Don't tell people they have been specially chosen for a gift, or that they might be one of a lucky sample to receive a gift – they are wise to this by now, having never ever had a gift, or if they have it is one that is binned.

It is often useful to produce two or three different designs to use in the testing stage. Check that everything will remain within the budget when reproduced on its full scale.

5. Test the mailing

Send out a copy of the mailing to a sample from the list (making sure your sample is large enough to yield valid results – the more you want to break it down into categories, the larger it needs to be). If more than one design of mailing was produced these should be tested. Evaluate the results by checking the time taken to reply, the information obtained, and subsequently the number of sales. Look for any sectors that have not replied, for example the younger age range.

6. Make modifications and produce the package

Make any necessary changes (which are identified from any confusion or doubts arising from the test) to the mailing and package. Have the final copy of the package printed to the numbers required.

7. Prepare for response

Plan for a maximum response. This may mean taking on additional staff temporarily or ordering greater levels of stock. Customers will not be happy if their order cannot be met and are told an item is sold out. Ensure staff are aware of the pending campaign and the possibility of a large response over a short period of time. Prepare to monitor increases in telephone calls, orders, or service usage.

8. Send out the mailing

Depending on the size of the mailing it is often sensible to outsource enve-lope-stuffing to an external agency. The size and importance of the mailing and the capability of existing resources and budgets will determine whether you need to take on temporary staff or not.

9. Evaluate the results

Look for the same pointers as in the test mailing, along with the capability of staff to cope with the increased workload. Check that the stimulus for early response worked. Compare the results of the campaign, for example numbers of extra sales, against the original objectives or targets. Overall, identify problem areas and ways that improvements could be made for next time. Make as much use as possible of the incoming data in order to improve your own customer databases and the profiles of order prospects.

Dos and don'ts for using direct mail

Do

- Use the most up-to-date and accurate mailing list you can obtain.
- Try to be innovative when designing your letter – but keep it short and to the point.
- Make sure the recipient knows what they have to do next.
- Offer a stimulus to reply quickly.
- Review the results and use them when planning future mailings.

Don't

- Send out the mailing without testing it on a sample first.
- Throw too much information at the addressee.
- Use language/terminology that the addressee will not understand.
- Forget that a successful campaign will increase the workload.

Useful reading

BOOKS

Successful direct mail in a week, Liz Ferdi, London: Hodder & Stoughton, 1995
How to write letters that sell, Christian Godfrey and Dominique Glocheux, London: Piatkus, 1995
The Royal Mail direct mail handbook, Les Andrews (editor), Watford: Exley, 1988

JOURNAL ARTICLES

How to write a letter that sells, Small Business Confidential, No 104, April 1992, pp8–10
It's in the post, Phil Churchill, Accountancy, Vol 104 no 1155, 1989, pp127–128
Making the most of mail campaigns, Winston Marsh, Australian Accountant, October 1989, pp28–31

Useful addresses

Direct Mail Department, Royal Mail Streamline, Streamline House, Sandylane West, Oxford, OX4 5ZZ, Tel: 01865 748768

Direct Marketing Association (UK) Ltd, Haymarket House, 1 Oxendon Street, London, SW1Y 4EE, Tel: 0171 321 2525

Effective Communications: Preparing Presentations

This checklist is intended for those who are required to give any form of presentation. It covers all the stages of preparing a talk, from accepting the invitation to checking the venue: the delivery of the presentation itself is covered in the following checklist (Effective Communications: Delivering Presentations). This checklist concentrates on how to develop an effective personal style rather than on the preparation of visual aids.

MCI Standards

This checklist has relevance for the MCI Management Standards: Key Role D – Manage Information.

Definition

For the purposes of this checklist, a presentation covers any talk to a group, whether formal or informal, from giving a team briefing to delivering a major speech: the same rules and principles apply.

Action checklist

1. Decide whether to accept

Ask yourself whether you are the right person to deliver this presentation. Do you have enough time to prepare? You may need to allow between 30 and 60 minutes for every minute of delivery. Are you excited enough about the topic to be enthusiastic? Do you know enough to answer awkward questions? If not, say no!

2. Clarify the details

Find out how long you will speak for and the exact subject. Will there be questions at the end? If there are other speakers, what will they cover, and how will you fit in with them?

3. Research your audience

View the audience as your customers. Try to gain a notion of their expectations: do they want to be informed, amused or challenged? How many will there be; what is their level and background; do they have any prior knowledge?

4. Define the purpose

Tailor the presentation to meet the audience needs you identified. Is the aim of the presentation to:

● persuade – a sales pitch
● instruct – if you know your topic
● inspire – as part of a change programme
● entertain – if you are naturally funny.

5. Assemble your material

Assemble anything relevant to your topic: ideas; articles; quotes; anecdotes; references. Accumulate the material over time but don't attempt to organise it while you collect it.

6. Organise your material

Review your collection. Group items into themes and topics. Are there metaphors or analogies which keep appearing?

7. Prepare an 'essay plan'

Structure the material into a rough plan. Aim for a beginning, a middle and an end.

8. Write a rough draft

Use the essay plan to sketch a first draft. Write without stopping and don't impose a structure while writing. Aim to tell the audience what you are going to say: tell them and end by summarising what you have told them. Try to make only five key points and a maximum of seven.

9. Edit the draft

Sleep on your first draft. Review it the following day. Convert the written word to speech: make the text more concrete, simpler and more illustrative. Use anecdotes. Shorten all your sentences and eliminate non-essential ideas and words. Cut any jargon or explain any that is unavoidable. Make sure the timing is right – speaking to an audience is slower than talking to a friend.

10. Refine the draft

Run through the draft several times, preferably in front of someone. Seek feedback and criticism on content, style and delivery. Ask your listener not to interrupt but to make notes.

11. Select your prompts

If you want or need to deliver a spontaneous presentation, run through the draft again and begin to highlight prompts – key words and phrases. These will be the basis of your script and perhaps your visual aids. Practise using the prompts alone and learn the thoughts behind the words. When you are confident, transfer the prompts to numbered cards. Continue practising and reducing the number of key words. (Sometimes, you will need to use a full script, for example, if the press are present, or if the occasion is very formal).

12. Select appropriate presentation aids

Presentation aids need to:

- be integrated – flow from your natural style
- move the presentation on – add value to it and be clearly relevant to content, or summarise what you are saying thus dispensing with a script
- be professional – clear, readable and consistent
- be appropriate in tone – full colour slides may not be right for a small informal group
- be simple to understand – clearly legible from the back of the room
- be graphic where appropriate – use symbols, drawings and charts to reinforce your words.

An increasing range of presentation aids, from flip charts and overhead transparencies to multimedia and computer generated graphics, is available.

13. Rehearse

Practise in your head, in front of a mirror or in front of a partner – he or she will be your sternest critic! Note any mannerisms you need to correct or anything you need constantly to remind yourself of as you talk: 'Don't put your hands in pockets!', 'Smile!'. Keep these on a cue card when you give the presentation.

14. Check the venue

Sit where the audience will sit and check your visuals are visible. Sit or stand where you will deliver the presentation and check you can work the equipment. Can you use the microphone?

Dos and don'ts for preparing effective presentations

Do

- Practise as much as possible. Seek feedback and be open to criticism.
- Constantly review the purpose of your presentation against the text: are you meeting the customer's expectations?
- Remember that thorough preparation is a key factor in minimising nerves and ensuring a successful presentation.
- Put some enthusiasm into your presentation – stimulate the audience.

Don't

- Sit in a room with a blank sheet of paper and try to write: look for external stimuli.
- Use a visual aid just because it is funny or striking and you can't bear to leave it out.
- Take anything for granted: the topic; the audience; the extent of their knowledge; the venue; the equipment.

Useful reading

Successful presentation in a week, 2nd ed, Malcolm Peel, London: Hodder & Stoughton, 1998

I hate giving presentations: your essential confidence booster, Michael D Owen, Ely: Fenman, 1997

Making successful presentations, Patrick Forsyth, London: Sheldon Press, 1995

Successful Presentations, Carole McKenzie, London: Century Business, 1993

The Perfect Presentation, Andrew Leigh and Michael Maynard, London: Century Business, 1993

Janner's Complete Speechmaker, 4th ed, Greville Janner QC MP, London: Business Books Ltd UK, 1991

Thought starters

- Have you agreed to speak just because you were asked: if so, do you really know and care enough about the topic to excite your audience?
- Are you trying to convey too much information in one presentation? Your audience will only absorb a maximum of seven key points.

Effective Communications: Delivering Presentations

This checklist is intended for anyone giving a presentation, whether formal or informal. It assumes that you have spent time in preparing an effective presentation (see the previous checklist Effective Communications: Preparing Presentations) and are now ready to deliver it.

MCI Standards

This checklist has relevance for the MCI Management Standards: Key Role D – Manage Information.

Definition

For the purposes of this checklist, a presentation covers any talk to a group, whether formal or informal, from giving a team briefing to delivering a major speech: the same rules and principles apply.

Action checklist

1. Choose the right style

The size of your audience and the purpose of the presentation will determine its style. Obtain precise information about audience size: a large audience for one presenter is but a small group to another.

- For five to ten, aim for an informal style with few visual aids. Sit or balance on the edge of a table or desk. Plan to establish relationships immediately and engage each individual.
- For ten to thirty, you need a more formal style but you can still establish relationships. Stand up and expect to use some visual aids.
- For thirty to a hundred, you will need good presentation aids and a formal style; it will be difficult to engage with individuals.

- Over a hundred, view this as a theatre style presentation: you will be 'on stage' and performing with a microphone. Your facial gestures and body language will need to be exaggerated to be effective.

2. Check the venue

Do a last minute check on equipment: can you use the microphone, the projector, are your visual aids visible? Who will introduce you and when? Is there a glass of water to hand?

3. Check your appearance

Ensure your appearance doesn't detract from your message. Dress conservatively and tidily. Check your tie, shoes, make-up.

4. Establish your presence

Once you have been introduced, pause; take a deep breath; look at the audience; make eye contact and acknowledge their presence. Relax your body and stand tall. Smile!

5. Establish your credentials

Explain why you are there and what gives you the authority to speak. Confirm the audience's expectations by announcing what you will speak about. Resolve any confusions or queries immediately: it is always possible you are in the wrong place!

6. Involve your audience

Get their attention initially using a visual aid or something unexpected. Ask a question, even if it is rhetorical. Say something that shows you understand their concerns or expectations. Deflecting attention to the audience removes some of the attention from you and helps with stage fright.

7. Let your personality show

Remember that feelings, not facts, convince people. Put genuine conviction behind what you are saying and allow your emotions to show through. This will also help you to overcome stage fright.

8. Use positive body language

Remember to stand erect. Don't lean on the lectern and don't play with your hair, tie, jewellery or clothing. For those who talk better on the move, walk around naturally and use your hands as you would in conversation for emphasis. Use ordinary facial expressions and, where appropriate, smile!

9. Take control of your voice

Project your voice through standing straight and breathing deeply. Speak clearly and more slowly than usual. Speak naturally but lower the pitch of your voice if you are nervous. Be aware of your speech mannerisms and consciously avoid repeating them. Avoid hesitating: if you have lost your place or your nerve, just pause, but don't 'um' or 'er'.

10. Introduce variety

Vary the timing of your delivery and the pitch of your voice. Speed up or slow down and change tone in different sections. Use inflections and emphases even if they sound exaggerated to you. Occasionally pause or stop completely in a long presentation – the audience need time to absorb the content and you need time to reflect: are you going too quickly; have you put your hands in your pockets without realising it?

11. Build on your rapport with the audience

Maintain eye contact and play to the cheerleaders – people you know or sense to be sympathetic. Show how your presentation is relevant to them and avoid using 'I' or 'me' too often.

12. Introduce humour

If you are confident, use humour to lighten or vary the mood. Use it only to support the text, not in its own right. Don't be cruel to anyone in the audience.

13. Face up to the unexpected

The audience will notice disturbances or mistakes but you will only remember how you handled them. Acknowledge rather than ignore interruptions and try to deflect or make light of them through humour.

14. Improvise

Although thorough preparation is essential it may be inappropriate to come over as too 'prepared', slick or clinical. Remember to adjust to the mood and atmosphere of the audience.

15. Conclude

Bring the presentation to a conclusion. Be brief, don't repeat the main text and end on a high, in tone, energy and content. Leave the audience wanting slightly more.

16. Be positive about questions

Actively encourage questions. Repeat the question so everyone can hear it. If you don't know the answer, admit it but offer to take a name and address to reply to later. Don't get into debate or argument.

Dos and don'ts for delivering effective presentations

Do

- Be yourself: allow your own personality to come through rather than trying to emulate presenters you admire.
- Start and finish on time – or before time if there are to be questions – otherwise you will lose the audience's sympathy regardless of how good the content is.
- Use handouts to convey detailed or complex ideas rather than cramming them into your presentation.

Don't

- Try to cover too much in one presentation and end up rushing to finish by talking faster.
- Use humour inappropriately or use it against your audience: you are the only legitimate target in the room.
- Use too many visual aids: they distract the audience and rarely add value.

Useful reading

Successful presentation in a week, 2nd ed, Malcolm Peel, London: Hodder and Stoughton, 1998

I hate giving presentations: your essential confidence booster, Michael D Owen, Ely: Fenman, 1997

Making successful presentations, Patrick Forsyth, London: Sheldon Press, 1995

The perfect presentation, Andrew Leigh and Michael Maynard, London: Century Business, 1993

Successful presentations, Carole McKenzie, London: Century Business, 1993

Janner's complete speechmaker, 4th ed, Greville Janner QC MP, London: Business Books Ltd, 1991

Thought starters

- Does each part of the content of your speech match up to the title and purpose?
- Do all your visual aids really add something to the spoken word?
- Have you tried your presentation out on guinea pigs for length, humour or interest?
- Have you ever used the particular visual aid you will be working with before?
- Do you know who your audience will be or how many there will be?

Performing a SWOT Analysis

This checklist is for those carrying out, or participating in, a SWOT analysis, SWOT being the acronym for Strengths Weaknesses Opportunities Threats. It is a simple, popular technique which can be used in preparing or amending plans, in problem solving and decision making, or for making staff generally aware of the need for change. The usefulness of SWOT analysis, however, has recently been questioned and may be seen as an outdated technique.

MCI standards

SWOT analysis has relevance for the MCI Management Standards: Key Role A – Manage Activities.

Definition

SWOT analysis is a general technique which can find suitable applications across diverse management functions and activities, but it is particularly appropriate to the early stages of strategic and marketing planning.

Performing a SWOT analysis involves the generation and recording of the strengths, weaknesses, opportunities, and threats concerning a task, individual, department, or organisation. It is customary for the analysis to take account of internal resources and capabilities (strengths and weakness) and factors external to the organisation (opportunities and threats).

Benefits

SWOT analysis can provide:

- a framework for identifying and analysing strengths, weaknesses, opportunities and threats
- an impetus to analyse a situation and develop suitable strategies and tactics
- a basis for assessing core capabilities and competences
- the evidence for, and cultural key to, change
- a stimulus to participation in a group experience.

Concerns

Hill and Westbrook argue that SWOT analysis is an overview approach which is unsuited to today's diverse and unstable markets. They also suggest that it can be ineffective as a means of analysis because of:

- the generation of long lists
- the use of description, rather than analysis
- a failure to prioritise
- a failure to use it in the later stages of the planning and implementation process.

Action checklist

1. Establish the objectives

The first key step in any management project: be clear on what you are doing and why. The purpose of conducting a SWOT may be wide or narrow, general or specific – anything from getting staff to understand, think about and be more involved in the business, to re-thinking a strategy, or even re-thinking the direction of the business.

2. Select appropriate contributors

Important if the final recommendations are to result from consultation and discussion, not just personal views, however expert.

- Pick a mix of specialist and 'ideas' people with the ability and enthusiasm to contribute.
- Consider how appropriate it would be to mix staff of different grades.
- Think about numbers. 6–10 people may be enough, especially in a SWOT workshop, but up to 25 or 30 can be useful if one of the aims is to get staff to see the need for change.

3. Allocate research and information gathering tasks

Background preparation is a vital stage for the subsequent analysis to be effective, and should be divided among the SWOT participants. This preparation can be carried out in two stages: exploratory, followed by data collection, and detailed, followed by a focused analysis.

- Gathering information on Strengths and Weaknesses should focus on the internal factors of skills, resources and assets, or lack of them.
- Gathering information on Opportunities and Threats should focus on the external factors over which you have little or no control, such as social, market or economic trends.

4. Create a workshop environment

If compiling and recording the SWOT lists takes place in meetings, then do exploit the benefits of workshop sessions. Encourage an atmosphere conducive to the free flow of information and to participants saying what they feel to be appropriate, free from blame. The leader / facilitator has a key role and should allow time for free flow of thought, but not too much. Half an hour is often enough to spend, for example, on Strengths, before moving on. It is important to be specific, evaluative and analytical at the stage of compiling and recording the SWOT lists – mere description is not enough.

5. List Strengths

Strengths can relate to the organisation, to the environment, to public relations and perceptions, to market shares, and to people. 'People' elements include the skills, capabilities and knowledge of staff which can provide a competitive edge, as well as reasons for past successes. Other people strengths include:

- friendly, cooperative and supportive staff
- a staff development and training scheme
- appropriate levels of involvement through delegation and trust.

'Organisation' elements include:

- customer loyalty
- capital investment and a strong balance sheet
- effective cost control programmes
- efficient procedures, systems and well-developed social responsibility.

6. List Weaknesses

This session should not constitute an opportunity to slate the organisation but be an honest appraisal of the way things are. Key questions include:

- What obstacles prevent progress?
- Which elements need strengthening?
- Where are the complaints coming from?
- Are there any real weak links in the chain?

The list for action could include:

- lack of new products or services
- declining market for main product
- poor competitiveness and higher prices
- non-compliance with, or non-awareness of, appropriate legislation
- lack of awareness of mission, objectives and policies
- regular staff absence
- absence of method for monitoring success or failure.

It is not unusual for 'People' problems – poor communication, inadequate leadership, lack of motivation, too little delegation, no trust, the left hand never knowing what the right is doing – to feature among the major weaknesses.

7. List Opportunities

This step is designed to assess the socio-economic, political, environmental and demographic factors, among others, to evaluate the benefits they may bring to the organisation. Examples include:

- the availability of new technology
- new markets
- a new government
- new programmes for training or monitoring quality
- changes in interest rates
- an ageing population
- strengths and weaknesses of competitors.

Bear in mind just how long opportunities might last and how the organisation may take best advantage of them.

8. List Threats

The opposite of Opportunities – all the above may, with a shift of emphasis or perception, have an adverse impact. Other threats may include:

- the level of unemployment
- environmental legislation
- an obsolete product range.

It is important to have a worst-case scenario. Weighing threats against opportunities is not a reason to indulge in pessimism; it is rather a question of considering how possible damage may be limited or eliminated. The same factors may emerge as both a threat and an opportunity, for example, Information Technology. Most external factors are in fact challenges, and whether staff perceive them as opportunities or threats is often a valuable indicator of morale.

9. Evaluate listed ideas against Objectives

With the lists compiled, sort and group facts and ideas in relation to the objectives. It may be necessary for the SWOT participants to select their five most important items from the list in order to gain a wider view. Clarity of objectives is key to this process, as evaluation and elimination will be necessary to cull the wheat from the chaff. Although some aspects may require further information or research, a clear picture should, at this stage, start to emerge in response to the objectives.

Make sure that the SWOT analysis is used in subsequent planning. Revisit your findings at suitable time intervals to check that they are still valid.

Dos and don'ts for SWOT analysis

Do

- Be analytical and specific.
- Record all thoughts and ideas in stages 5-8.
- Be selective in the final report.
- Choose the right people for the exercise.
- Choose a suitable SWOT leader or facilitator.

Don't

- Try to disguise weaknesses.
- Merely list errors and mistakes.
- Lose sight of external influences and trends.
- Allow the SWOT to become a blame-laying exercise.
- Ignore the outcomes at later stages of the planning process.

Useful reading

JOURNAL ARTICLES

SWOT Analysis: it's time for a product recall, Terry Hill and Ray Westbrook, Long Range Planning, vol 30 no 1, February 1997, pp46–52

A framework for analysing service operations, Gabriel R Bitran and Maureen Lojo, European Management Journal, vol 11 no 3, September 1993, pp271–282

It pays to analyse your strengths and weaknesses, Small Business Confidential, no 57, May 1988, pp7–8

TRAINING PACKAGE

Identifying strengths, weaknesses, opportunities and threats, CBT package from Maxim Training Systems, 61 Ship Street, Brighton, BN1 1AE, Tel: 01273 204198

Report Writing

> **This checklist is intended both for those new to report writing and for experienced report writers who wish to review their own methods.**

MCI Standards

This checklist has relevance for the MCI Management Standards: Key Role D – Manage Information.

Definition

A good report should be readable, interesting and well presented, and it should be no longer than is necessary. It keeps the needs of the readership clearly in mind. As the readers are likely to be busy people who already have a problem reading the material that passes through their hands, a verbose and lengthy document is unlikely to be welcome. A good structure, with clear conclusions and a summary, is vital if an acceptable document is to be produced.

Advantages of good report writing

- Helps you to communicate more effectively.
- Improves your status and your career prospects.
- Contributes to business success by improving communication.
- Creates a good corporate image of the organisation.
- Greatly assists the process of planning and decision making.

Disadvantages of poor report writing

- Time is wasted as readers search for the information they require.
- Readers are frustrated because the information provided is incomplete.
- Misunderstandings result from the lack of clarity in the language used.
- A lack of confidence is felt in both the writer and the message they are trying to put across.
- The report is not read at all.

Action checklist

1. Preparation

Putting pen to paper (or fingers to keyboard) is not the way to start the report writing process. You have to plan what you are going to produce if you want to produce an effective document. In preparing for the actual writing process you should:

- consider the terms of reference or precise purpose. They should define why the report is needed, the type of report it should be, the scope of the subject that is to be covered, and the time scale.
- identify the readership. Is the person who requested the report the primary reader? Who else will see the report? What can the readers be expected to know about the subject? What do they need to know about the subject?
- establish the objectives in your own terms. Present as results to be achieved rather than intentions.

2. Gather and collate the information

With most reports you will not have all the information needed to hand so some form of research or data collection will be required. This may entail identifying and reading other reports, interviewing people, carrying out primary research or drawing together data from a number of different locations. Gathering too much information is not a bad fault; gathering too little definitely is – but bear in mind what you want the information for, otherwise you can bury yourself in a mound of data. Reports are far easier to write when you are able to choose from the information immediately to hand. The important thing is to gain a balanced picture of the subject.

3. Structure your report

Analyse the information to identify that which is most important and that which provides supporting evidence. To achieve this you need to refer back to your terms of reference and your readership. With long documents a detailed outline will be needed. This should link the main subjects with the topics they cover. Consider the order in which you are presenting the information. Restructure them if the order does not seem logical and it fails to portray the message you want.

Plan the layout of your report following the house style of your organisation if applicable. A simple framework for a format can form the basis of most reports. This should include:

- Introduction (to include terms of reference and the methodology)
- Summary
- Main report
- Conclusions

- Recommendations
- Supplementary evidence (including full tables and figures which would obstruct the reading of the main report)

4. Write the report

View your first attempt at putting the report together as a draft. Your plan will provide a broad picture of what you want to achieve. By writing in a single sitting you are far more likely to retain your original concept. Setting yourself a deadline can help to focus the mind.

Make your writing as persuasive as possible by:

- keeping your message simple without oversimplifying
- writing positively, as negative statements are not so easy to understand
- using the active voice, as it is easier to understand than the passive
- including only the information the reader needs to know
- avoiding long and complex sentences, especially those with several subordinate clauses
- using long words only when they are appropriate
- using short words and phrases for conciseness and clarity
- employing technical terms only where they are unavoidable or where you are sure that your audience will understand them. A glossary may be required to assist your readers.

Graphics and visuals are invaluable for expressing complex information. The forms available include tables, line graphs, bar graphs, divided bar graphs, pie charts, pictographs and illustrations; figures are generally to be preferred to tables of data. They should be formatted with care, clearly numbered and titled and introduced within the text. If the graphic is included to help explain a key point it should be placed as close to that point as possible. If it is supplied for documentary support it can be placed at the end of the report. It is often useful to include a simplified or summary figure or table in the main report and to relegate detailed data to an appendix.

5. Review what you have written

You should always allow time to review what you have written, but this should not be done as soon as you have finished writing. Starting the revision a day or two after can be more effective as the ideas are still clear in your mind, but you are fresher to analyse critically what you have written and can view it with more perspective. You will often find simpler and shorter ways of saying what you intend.

Consider whether the report says what you want it to say. Does it fully cover the terms of reference? Analyse the readability of the report, making use of such techniques as Gunning's Fog Index. Check the structure of the report. Check spelling, punctuation and grammatical correctness.

Do your conclusions sufficiently differentiate between those drawn from information presented in the report, your own personal comments and recommendations as to future action based on the report findings?

Ask a colleague to proof-read the report and to consider issues such as ease of understanding and structure.

6. Printing and submission

House style may dictate how your report should be printed and should be followed. For guidance the layout should allow generous margins and make use of a readable typeface. For longer reports starting each section on a new page is advisable.

Aim to submit your report ahead of schedule.

Dos and don'ts for report writing

Do
- Express clearly and concisely what you have to say.
- Provide a summary of the main issues and conclusions.
- Be complete.
- Write with a clear idea of your readership.
- Write with a clear idea of what you are aiming to achieve.

Don't
- Write to impress.
- Include information only because you have found it.

Useful reading

How to write effective reports, 3rd ed, John E Sussams, Aldershot: Gower, 1998

No sweat! The indispensable guide to reports and dissertations, Ray Irving and Cathy Smith, Corby: Institute of Management Foundation, 1998

Persuasive reports and proposals, Andrew Leigh, London: Institute of Personnel and Development, 1997

Successful report writing in a week, Katharine Hertiage, London: Hodder & Stoughton, 1997

Thought starters

- When does the report have to be submitted?
- Who is the readership?
- What information do you need?
- Do you understand the brief for the report?
- Should you be following a house style?

Handling Complaints

This checklist outlines a procedure for handling complaints in small or large, manufacturing or service, private or public sector organisations.

It is designed to enable a consistent organisation-wide approach to complaints which ensures that they are dealt with effectively to the advantage of both the customer and the organisation.

MCI Standards

This checklist has relevance for the MCI Management Standards: Key Role A – Manage Activities.

Definition

A complaint is an expression of lack of satisfaction with any product or service, whether orally or in writing, from an internal or external customer.

Advantages

A complaints procedure:

- provides a clear approach when a complaint occurs
- engenders understanding and confidence on how to tackle complaints
- helps to remove personal 'guilt' feelings when receiving a complaint
- leads to a recognition of complaints as valuable feedback, not criticisms
- can produce records for analysing possible service improvements.

Action checklist

1. Establish a common approach to handling complaints

This must have widespread approval from the top to the bottom of the organisation, including staff who do not come into direct contact with customers. Ensure that everyone is thinking about customers in the same way. This should be embedded into the organisation's culture and is primarily the responsibility of senior management.

Remember that when customers complain, they like to be:

- aware of who is dealing with the complaint

- listened to and believed
- treated fairly and efficiently
- kept informed of progress
- compensated if it is appropriate.

2. Draw up a standard complaints form

This is a valuable tool which should include the following sub-headings:

Receipt details
- date received
- received by
- department/division

Customer details
- name, address, identifier
- telephone / fax / e-mail

Complaint details

Action (to be) taken
- date completed
- sign-off
- line superior

3. Ensure complaints are assessed correctly

On receipt of a complaint, the recipient should look on it as a second chance to satisfy the customer. Staff should:

- be courteous and empathise with the customer
- ensure that all the details are obtained and recorded on the standard complaints form
- be satisfied that the information is factual
- not admit liability or fault at this stage.

Subject to appropriate information seeking and establishment of the facts, the recipient, in conjunction with his or her line manager if necessary, should decide whether it is a major or minor complaint.

Minor complaints may result from misinterpretation, misunderstanding, detail errors, or straightforward carelessness. Major complaints may involve breach of the criminal law or have health and safety or financial implications.

4. Establish ownership and responsibility

Staff should be empowered to take appropriate action if the complaint is clearly justified, falls within their jurisdiction, and can be rectified immediately. If the complaint cannot be resolved by the recipient, details of the customer and complaint should be noted on the form and passed quickly to the relevant area or level of responsibility. The customer should be told who is dealing with the complaint – nothing is more frustrating than dealing with a faceless organisation, or being passed from one person to another – and that a reply will be given as soon as possible, and within a specified time limit.

5. Establish escalation procedures

In the case of major complaints, the manager should decide on the appropriate action and this may involve:

- consulting a higher authority
- the production of a detailed report on the events
- contact with the organisation's solicitor
- contact with the police.

6. Emphasise customer contact for complaint resolution

If the level of seriousness has been properly understood, and the establishment of the facts correctly carried out, then appropriate action should become apparent. Problem resolution is not a time for negotiation or bartering with a customer who has a genuine grievance and who should perhaps be compensated generously. If there is any delay in resolving complaints, the customer should be contacted at regular, agreed intervals so that a progress update can be given.

7. Ensure complaints forms are signed off

When the problem has been resolved to the satisfaction of the customer, the recipient or superior should sign off the complaints form for subsequent analysis of any complaints trends.

It could be that there is no satisfactory solution, that the customer may require something 'unreasonable' or 'beyond' the remit of the organisation to deliver. If this occurs, it may be appropriate to:

- inform the customer that expectations exceeded capabilities
- re-affirm which steps can be taken
- and to state that a report will be passed on to senior management.

8. Decide internal corrective action

Having dealt with the complaint, decide whether any system, equipment or personnel-related improvement needs tackling. Deal with internal process improvements or training requirements as soon as possible after the complaint has occurred.

9. Build in customer satisfaction checks

After an appropriate interval, say two weeks, get back in touch with the customer to confirm that the complaint was satisfactorily resolved – and to check that the organisation still has a customer.

10. Analyse complaints periodically

All complaints forms should be returned to a simple, central address where a manager should have responsibility for monitoring the level and nature of complaints on a regular basis. The results of this analysis, and details of any corrective action, should be reported to senior management on a regular basis.

Dos and don'ts for handling complaints

Do
- Make customer service part of the corporate culture.
- Empower staff to deal with complaints.
- Keep in contact with the customer to ensure that the complaint is dealt with to their satisfaction.
- Analyse the pattern of complaints and take action to make improvements.
- Treat complaints positively.

Courtesy, speed of response and a personal touch are essential. A complaining customer who gets all three will usually emerge a more satisfied customer than before he/she had any complaints. And he/she will tell others in turn.

Don't allow staff to:
- blame the computer
- say it's not their department
- take the complaint personally or defensively
- allocate blame
- use paperwork to block a fast response to complaints.

Offhandedness, slowness and impersonality are likely to lose you not only that customer but many others as well – bad news spreads.

Useful reading

Books

Dealing with demanding customers: how to turn complaints into opportunities, David M Martin and Institute of Management, London: Pitman, 1994

Tough talking: how to handle awkward situations, David M Martin and Institute of Management, London: Pitman, 1993

JOURNAL ARTICLES

How to handle complaints successfully, Winston Marsh, Australian Accountant, May 1990, pp26–30

Customer-focused re-engineering in Telstra: corporate complaints handling in Australia, Virginia Bendall-Harris, Business Change and Re-engineering, Vol 2 no 1, 1994, pp7–14

Employee complaints: act early and be concerned, Henry J Pratt, ARMA Records Management Quarterly, Vol 23 no 1, January 1989, pp26–28

Thought starters

- Do staff know what to do when they receive a complaint?
- Does the organisation receive many complaints?
- Does it receive many different kinds of complaints?
- Are they recorded?
- What happens to the records?
- When you last complained, how was it dealt with? Have you used that organisation again?
- An organisation that never has any complaints is probably a bad one – no one bothers to complain, they just go elsewhere.

Networking

This checklist is designed to help you to develop your business networking skills, in order to retain and gain customers and suppliers, and to expand your range of beneficial contacts.

MCI Standards

This checklist has relevance for the MCI Management Standards: Key Roles A and B – Manage Activities and Manage Resources.

Definition

The term 'networking' produces different responses from different people. As an activity, networking is not new. It is a well-established activity which has attracted a new label.

Our networks embrace the range of informal and formal relationships in which we are involved; networking implies an awareness of our networks and of their potential value both to ourselves and to other members.

Networks overlap; A and B may be in the same network but each will have contacts in other networks. Our networks are not static – if we use them, they constantly expand, but if we neglect them, they shrink.

Networks are generally of four kinds – personal, organisational, professional and strategic. All provide access to information, development opportunities, support and influence.

Benefits of networking

Networking enables you to:

- improve and extend the quality of your relationships
- create opportunities to meet more potential customers
- be better informed and share information with fellow network members
- share in your customers' social interests, thus enhancing your business relationships
- meet your peers in other organisations.

Disadvantages of networking

Networks don't just happen: they require the investment of those rare commodities, time and energy. They also require a disposition to give as well as take. Most of us are happy to do this; for the minority who are not, networking may be an embarrassment.

Action checklist

1. Prepare for your networking

Networking is an activity and a skill which requires planning if it is to succeed. Remember the aim of networking (in the present context) is to improve your business potential. Spend some time identifying networks of which you would like to be a member. Are you interested in 'talking shops' which may be sources of new contacts, or in situations which may provide opportunities for self-development, or as a step on the road to the development of your business?

2. Identify formal networks and develop relationships with them

Professional Institutes and Associations run local activities and help you to keep up-to-date with technical developments. They inform you about successes and 'best practice' in your line of business and provide support for your continuing professional development.

Trade Associations help you to keep up-to-date with new products and industry trends, and can help to identify opportunities for the future.

Training and Enterprise Councils (TECs)/Local Enterprise Companies (LECs) are bodies with remits to develop training and expertise in their local areas. The objectives of TECs usually include securing the commitment of employers to improve the education and training of their employees and to foster enterprise in the local community. Management Development meetings organised by TECs are usually free of charge, and business expansion advice is also readily available.

Business Links aim to improve the competitiveness of local firms by bringing together local support organisations, such as TECs and Chambers of Commerce, to develop the full range of services focused on customer needs and delivered from a single point of access. Personal Business Advisers will visit you and help you to plan the development and running of your business. Some services are free of charge. Open meetings encourage business people to get together.

Business Clubs are often focused on small businesses, where members have similar ideas and problems. Meetings are usually informal and activities promote contact between members to generate business between them.

Chambers of Industry and Commerce provide information on a wide range of business activities in your area. Chambers have links with Training and Enterprise Councils/Local Enterprise Companies, Business Links and the Department of Trade and Industry. They hold social events to help you establish and build on personal relationships with customers and suppliers. Many local Chambers offer continuous programmes of training courses and seminars.

3. Identify informal networks

These include:

- sports and social clubs
- neighbourhood organisations and community groups
- voluntary organisations.

The range of such organisations varies from town to town and from area to area.

4. Take steps to foster your networks

Consider what networks you belong to and the range of your contacts in each. Who could help you? Whom could you help? Build up a record to which you can refer. Consider how you propose to develop your networks.

Take stock. What do you want from your network? Are you looking for a regular flow of information, opportunities to develop yourself and your business, support, access to influence, or opportunities to become influential? What, in turn, can you contribute? What are you prepared to contribute?

Learn how to behave in ways that are consistent with networking ethics. Be open-minded; keep your promises; treat others in the way in which you would like to be treated; and ask for and give help without embarrassment. Most of all, don't forget to acknowledge help. A smile and a thank-you are beyond price.

How will you go about networking? What style of approach suits you best? Michelli and Straw suggest that there are three styles:

Conscious networkers have clear-cut goals. They recognise what is missing in their networks and set out to identify those who will meet their needs and to meet and develop relationships with them. The approach of conscious networkers is systematic and calculating.

Open networkers are again calculating but tend to take a longer-term view, building networks with the future in mind. Their objectives may be less clear-cut than those of intuitive networkers but they recognise those who may be useful in the future and cultivate relationships with them.

Intuitive networkers are neither systematic nor calculating. They enjoy mixing with people and do so as a matter of course. They are 'good with people' and may even be unaware of the extent of their range of contacts or of their potential value in a business context.

5. Get down to practicalities

● **Design your business card to project you and your business**
Think of all the factors – colour, logo, taste, positive messages – that will help to make people remember your business. There are two sides to your business card, so consider listing some of your services on the reverse side. If you export/import, carry bilingual cards – it will make it easier for your foreign customer/supplier to network with you.

● **Describe your business in a nutshell**
Prepare a clean, short, introductory statement which describes you and your business. If it's more than two sentences long you will lose the listener's attention. Adapt the statement to the person you are talking to – this will prevent it sounding too rehearsed. Use humour if you feel people will be comfortable. It can relax the atmosphere and encourage other people to join in the conversation. But do keep what you have to say brief – no one wants to listen to a long, tedious diatribe about how wonderful your business is. Be brief and let the facts speak for themselves.

● **Prepare a brochure**
If you prepare a brochure describing your products/services, make sure it is in plain English, free from jargon. Clear statements, with plenty of white space, are more effective than a cluttered brochure with lots of colour in it. Remember to convey the message – simply and straightforwardly – that you care about your customers and wish to meet their needs, not just to sell them what you have to offer.

● **Get to meetings/events in good time**
The sooner you get there, the more chance you have to arrange things to your advantage. If there is an opportunity to display your brochures, set out a few for people to pick up. If name badges are available, wear one. Having your own is useful, as event badges often use small print. When you are introduced to new people, let them do the talking to begin with. You will learn about them, what interests them, what is concerning them. Encourage them to talk about their business and their future plans. This information will help you to decide how to develop the new relationship. Don't stay too long with each person. Offer your business card, and suggest you might talk again later. Keep the other person's card in a separate pocket to the one in which you have yours, or you may find yourself handing out someone else's card.

- **Offer help**

Offer to help if you wish to meet someone again to discuss business. It signals a clear message of service, rather than of blatantly wanting a person's custom.

- **Listen to people's contributions**

Business presentations at meetings can be ideal for picking up a possible lead – people often express their problems to a group, rather than confide only in their business partners. You may also identify competitors who could benefit from a partnership arrangement.

- **Generate a record for each contact**

Set some time aside each week to chase up contacts – regular contact with people will encourage them to think about you and possibly steer business in your direction.

- **Make notes after informal meetings**

You can't easily make notes while talking to people, but you can often jot down a key word which you can expand on afterwards – immediately afterwards, while your memory is still fresh.

Useful reading

Networking (**Management Directions**), Dena Michelli and Fiona McWilliams, Corby: The Institute of Management Foundation, 1996

Successful networking in a week, Dena Michelli and Alison Straw, London: Hodder & Stoughton, 1995

Working for yourself: the Daily Telegraph guide to self-employment, 15th ed, Godfrey Golzen, London: Kogan Page, 1994

Thought starters

- People buy from people, so your customers are part of your network.
- Talk about their problems and how you can help; they don't want to know about yours.
- Recall some point from the last conversation you had with X. It may help X to remember you.

Using Your Bank to the Best Advantage

> This checklist makes practical suggestions to enable the customer to use a bank – or banks – to their best advantage, and it encourages the customer to see the relationship with their bank as one between equals and not one in which a supplicant is dispensed favours by the bank at its whim.
>
> Good relationships have always been important, but in a situation in which the high street banks are changing and streamlining their operating structures, they may be more difficult to establish and maintain. Today, the one-to-one relationship of the past between the owner of a business and a bank may no longer be entirely appropriate or easy to achieve. Therefore, a planned approach to relationships with your bank has become even more important than before.

MCI Standards

This checklist has relevance for the MCI Management Standards: Key Role B – Manage Resources.

Definition

'The bank' is the high street bank, building society, post office, financial institution or even supermarket where the customer's account(s) is (are) held. The customer may be corporate or private or both. The proprietor or manager will have a relationship with the bank on behalf of the business and may also have his personal account with the bank. 'The bank', as used here, does not include merchant or investment banks or other financial institutions providing services used only occasionally, if ever, by the average business.

Action checklist

1. Find out the structure within which the bank operates

The days when a branch of a high street bank was self-contained, with its own manager with clearly defined authority, have long since ceased. Today there are networks of geographically spread units with mobile specialists and a group or area manager who may not be located in your nearest branch. Nevertheless there will be a senior official with whom you normally deal, the focal point of your relationship with the bank. Find out from him or her the structure within which they operate. It will almost certainly be wider than your immediate town unless the branch is above average size.

Find out also the organisational structure within the building which you regard as the branch. Ask who does what; what functions are carried out elsewhere; and what authorities must be sought elsewhere. Above all, identify the official whom you should recognise as your 'bank manager'.

2. Get to know your bank(s) and be sure they get to know you

Keep your bankers informed, in advance, about developments or initiatives in your business. Do not appear to presume about the likely attitude of your bankers in any situation.

Aim to create a situation in which the person who deals with you will recognise you when you telephone the bank and will make that little extra effort to help which can mean so much. Ensure that neither of you is just a voice at the end of a telephone or a signature at the end of a letter, but a real person of whom each of you has a clear picture in mind.

The bank will want to form as complete a picture of your business as it can. Your colleagues and your staff are your best ambassadors. Invite your bank manager to visit your premises where they can meet each other. Give a short presentation about what the business does, who and where its customers are, and the structure within the business. Consider whether you should introduce someone as your deputy with whom the bank can deal in your absence.

3. Enquire about new or improved services which may be available

Keep in regular contact with your bankers as part of the process of promoting mutual familiarity. Enquire about changes in, and additions to, what the bank can provide as a service to your business. In these days of rapid technological development, changes can emerge without customers being aware of them, unless they make an effort to keep well informed. Find out about the pros and cons of:

- electronic banking
- distance banking
- direct debiting for making as well as receiving payments
- using BACS (the Bankers Automated Clearing System) for making and receiving payments directly into and out of your account
- methods of making foreign payments
- short-, medium- and long-term investments for available cash.

Using Your Bank to the Best Advantage

Try to forget the services you have used, perhaps for many years and take a fresh look at what services your bank offers. Obtain the bank's literature on the services currently available. Don't fall into the trap of assuming you know – you may not. Ask about products and services available through the bank – or associated organisations – such as:

- business credit cards
- insurance
- car fleet management
- debt factoring
- investment management.

4. Discuss changes and developments in your business with your bank

Be prudent and keep your bank informed. Ask what help they may be able to offer in your changing business. Don't think purely in terms of finance – term loans, shorter loans or an extended overdraft. Recognise that the services of today's banks extend far beyond the provision of funds into advice and help with planning and control, as well as services for holidays and foreign travel.

5. Discuss your business plans with the bank

You may or may not regularly prepare a business plan. Your bankers would prefer it if you did so. Conventional wisdom strongly supports the view that those with business plans are more likely to succeed than those who adopt Micawber management ('wait and see what turns up'). See Writing a Business Plan on page 17 for more details.

- Discuss your plan with your bankers – don't present it as a fait accompli, especially if it makes assumptions about the bank's attitude towards support for the business. Instead, present it as a document for discussion towards which bank thinking can make a valuable contribution.
- Be prepared to revise your draft plan in the light of comments, but be prepared to argue your case. You know your business better than anyone.
- Remember that the bank will be especially interested in cash flow and loan repayment.

6. Show periodic statements of results to the bank

It is one thing to have plans, another to achieve them. Show the bank your results, perhaps at the same time as you produce your new or revised business plan. These documents should, after all, dovetail. Invite comment and expect constructive criticism. Ask for suggestions for those parts of the business that require special attention. Present a schedule of your debtors and creditors and, in particular, highlight potential bad or doubtful debts. The bank is much more likely to help you if you have made it aware of likely difficulties in advance.

7. Keep your bankers informed in advance

Always consider the impact on the bank if a cheque, drawn by you, is presented when there are inadequate funds in your account to meet it. Remember that you may know that you will be paying in a deposit tomorrow which covers your cheque several times over, but your bankers do not. Remember that their concern may be the attitude of their 'head office' if they pay your cheque and end up embarrassed. Take your bankers into your confidence whenever the situation requires it and earn their trust.

8. Keep your promises

Don't make promises to the bank unless you are confident that you can meet them. The banker-customer relationship is one based on mutual confidence and trust. Don't undermine the relationship by carelessness.

It is easy to adopt a policy of telling the bank the good news and of omitting the things which you feel it may not wish to hear. The bank wishes (and needs) to hear the bad news as well as the good news.

9. Consider using two banks

Weigh up the pros and cons of using more than one bank. This may fit in with the geographical spread – actual or proposed – of your business. It may inspire each bank to seek the remainder of your business more actively and on more favourable terms. It may provide you with an alternative source of help if one bank decides that it cannot assist you in a particular situation.

Recognise that, whether you call it market research or 'shopping around', a good businessman will wish to be aware of what the range of high street banks is able to offer in the way of services. Visit them and ask – they will be glad to welcome you as a potential customer. Be sure to make your purpose clear and avoid leaving the impression that you are ready to close your account with X bank and to open an account with Y-Z bank.

Just as the bank will want to assess your business performance, so will you want to check out the bank, and look elsewhere if you are not satisfied.

10. View banks as organisations which want to do business with you

See banks as institutions seeking business and wanting you as a customer. Reject the traditional view of the bank as an institution dispensing favours – lending you money if you had money and not otherwise. Challenge the bank to do business with you. See it as a source of information and help, to be provided on a commercial basis, of course, but also on equal terms. Remember that bankers and businesses need each other.

Dos and don'ts for using your bank to the best advantage

Do

- See the bank as providing a package of services.
- Work at creating a relationship with your bankers which will enable you to take full advantage of all the services available.
- Keep yourself informed about developments in the banking sector as a whole.
- Show them your business as a complete entity, warts and all.
- Take them into your confidence and be completely frank with them, always as far in advance as possible.

Don't

- See banks only as a source of overdrafts – explore the whole range of services available.
- Overlook the possibility of having your private account in another bank to give you a 'foot in a second camp'.

Useful reading

BOOK

How to deal with your bank manager, Geoffrey Sales, London: Kogan Page, 1988

JOURNAL ARTICLES

Businessman's guide through the money maze, Malcolm Brown, Management Today, Nov 1995, pp128–130, 133–134

Your banks and how to choose them, Derek Ross, Accountancy, Nov vol 104 no 1155 1989, pp130, 132

The wooing bank, Andy Hunter, Certified Accountant, Dec 1989, pp36-38

How to get the bank managers eating out of your hand, Small Business Confidential, Feb no 6 1984, pp2–6

Useful address

Office of the Banking Ombudsman, 70 Gray's Inn Road, London WC1X 8NB, Tel: 0171 404 9944

Thought starters

- Your bankers declare 'they are happy with you'. Are you happy with your bankers?
- What bank services are available which you do not use?
- Don't you like your customers to keep you informed?
- What would you do if the bank suddenly said 'no'?

Preparing for Business Abroad

This checklist aims to stimulate thoughts about some of the implications of doing business abroad – of doing business with people of other nationalities, races and cultures. Success in doing business abroad often depends on 'getting the little things right' – recognising and anticipating cultural differences. The purpose of this checklist is to help you do that by pointing out some general guidelines and some specific examples. It is not a manual on foreign trade.

MCI Standards

This checklist has relevance for the MCI Management Standards: Key Role A – Manage Activities.

Definition

For the purposes of this checklist 'doing business abroad' involves either transacting business with people from other countries or transacting business in a country outside Britain. In doing business abroad you will be confronted with people of nationalities, races and cultures other than your own, and probably with customs, practices and legal systems which differ from yours.

Advantages of preparing for business abroad

It:

- increases your self-confidence in a situation which might be stressful
- enables you to appear informed and international in your outlook
- reduces the chances of your being taken by surprise by suddenly discovering that 'they' do things differently
- reduces the chances of you and your colleagues on the one hand, and of your potential business partners on the other, being embarrassed
- reduces the possibility of misunderstanding and increases the possibility of mutual understanding.

Action checklist

1. Identify sources of information

Write to, ring or even visit the embassy in Britain of the country you are visiting. Most have some literature about their countries which will provide useful background. In the case of some smaller countries, particularly those less economically developed, don't count on printed information being completely up-to-date.

Don't expect all embassy buildings to be like those of the United States or other major powers in the world. Some embassies consist of no more than two or three rooms on an upper floor. If you intend to visit an embassy, make a telephone call first to discover the hours during which it will be open to visitors. They are not all open 9.00am–5.00pm daily! In some embassies the staff will speak perfect English but in others they may not – be prepared for this if you speak to embassy staff on the telephone.

Once you are in the country which you are visiting, remember the British Embassy and, if it has an office in the country, the British Council, as sources of information.

Other sources of information include the Department of Trade and Industry, newspaper databases and the Financial Times' country profiles. And don't despise books intended for the tourist – they may contain useful information that is not available elsewhere (for example on tipping or good places to eat). The best source may be someone who has recently been to the country.

2. Decide what you need to know

- Find out the principal and minority languages of the country you are visiting. Mistaken assumptions can be embarrassing. Most countries in South America speak Spanish (with some differences which should not cause problems if you know Spanish) but Brazilians do not.

- Find out something about the history of the country you are visiting, especially its more recent history. In the case of the countries of Eastern Europe, recent histories may be complex but it is as well to know the influences which other countries may have had on the country in question.

- Discover whether there are significant minorities in the country. There are for example 600,000 ethnic Hungarians in Slovakia out of a population of 5 million. Their presence can have a major impact on the relationships between neighbours. Don't forget you may be attempting to do business with a member of a minority or mixed group.

- Discover something about your host country's internal politics but refrain from comment on them. It is impossible to know the alignment of your hosts and again in Eastern Europe and the states of the former USSR you must be careful. Many have adopted new political labels without changing their views, ambitions or allegiances.

- Discover something also about a country's religion. Many countries have more than one major religion although religious activity may be limited. Don't assume that all countries observe the same religious festivals as Britain or that they observe them in the same way or even on the same dates – many countries have a lot more public holidays than Britain, and you need to know when they are if you are not to find that some of your time in that country is wasted. Sundays are not always a 'day of rest' (cf Israel).

- Find out what temperatures and humidity are likely to be during your visit, so you can take suitable clothing.

3. Establish whether you need a visa

You may or may not need a visa – an authorisation, fixed or stamped in your passport, by your intended host country – in order to visit it. A travel agent can advise you on this, but it is often sensible to approach the embassy of your intended host. The embassy will issue a visa if you require one. Don't assume that you can obtain a visa instantly. You may need to fill in a very complex form; you may need to produce passport-size photographs; you will need to produce a valid passport. You may have to wait for several days; you may or may not have to pay for the visa. It is usually much quicker to go to the embassy in person than to do the transaction by mail.

4. Sort out foreign currency

Seek the advice of your bank or travel agent on what you should take. It may be possible to take some of your host country's currency but this is not always the case. Deutschmarks or US Dollars may be acceptable in the country you are visiting and travellers' cheques are a good stand-by.

It is probably advisable if you intend to take US Dollars only to take those issued during the last five years. Older ones are not acceptable in some countries where counterfeit dollars have been circulated in large numbers. Order currency in advance.

Unless you are a very experienced traveller, prepare a matrix giving at least approximate exchange cross rates of:

- the pound
- the local currency (know its subdivision)
- the US Dollar
- the Deutschmark
- the Japanese Yen.

Find out in advance whether, or which, credit cards you may use abroad; whether they are accepted in shops and restaurants; whether they can be used to obtain local currency at banks; whether they can be used in cash dispensers and:

- be prepared to pay a bank commission if you use your credit card to obtain currency
- be prepared to produce your passport at the same time if you want to avoid a journey back to your hotel
- don't obtain too much cash at once – find out in advance what your bank in Britain will accept if you bring foreign currency back (certainly not coins and possibly not notes from certain countries). Some countries do not permit you to take their currency out. Also, in countries with rapid inflation you can lose money by changing too much at once.

5. Find out about the local culture

As a starting point, check out the following aspects of culture:

- Tips – local custom may or may not require them. The amount and way of giving a tip (especially in a restaurant) may not follow our practice. Some require tips for taxis and not for restaurants, others vice-versa. Don't assume a standard rate of tipping applies across all services. In some countries expectations differ according to the area or city you are in (New York cab drivers expect 15%, in Chicago 10% will do.)
- Find out the locally acceptable practice for giving and receiving gifts.
- Don't be surprised by local toilet arrangements – mixed toilets supervised by a woman are not unknown. It is better to be prepared than shocked.
- Find out what is and what is not good manners. The belch which must be avoided at home may be obligatory in some countries to show appreciation of your host's cuisine. Some countries have unusual customs. In Norway, for example, if you are invited to a person's home for a meal, you are expected to make a speech afterwards praising the dinner and the hostess. People are sometimes very critical of their country – but can be offended if you agree with them.
- Find out about travel arrangements before you take a taxi or board a tram. It may be at least desirable to negotiate a taxi fare in advance. It may be necessary to purchase a tram ticket from a newsagent – and to cancel the ticket yourself on the tram. Find out about tickets first – and then watch the other passengers.
- Know something about the local police. Do they issue on-the-spot fines? For what?
- Be cautious about the local sense of humour. Few of us could describe our national or personal sense of humour. Some laugh at themselves; some only at their neighbours. Some who laugh at themselves don't like others to laugh at them.

- Learn about physical gestures – a nod in Bulgaria signifies lack of agreement.
- Don't make jokes about former communists or socialist institutions in Eastern Europe. You may be talking to a former communist about an institution which he managed. Only your order book may reflect his reaction.
- Accept hospitality carefully – 'pace it'. Your hosts may be used to whatever exotic drink you are taking – you may not.

Dos and don'ts in preparing for business abroad

Do

- Remember that people from other countries and cultures are as proud of their histories, cultures and achievements as you are.
- Remember the importance of listening.
- Know a few words in the language of your potential business partners – salutations especially.
- Try to know what is likely to be in the news headlines of the country during the period of your discussions and perhaps something of the background to those news items.
- Avoid religious issues.

Don't

- Patronise your contacts.
- Criticise the country's politicians – they may support them.
- Criticise the sanitary arrangements or standards of hygiene: just be grateful that you don't have to live with them.
- Make assumptions based on your standards, customs and practices.

Useful reading

Management worldwide, David J Hickson and Derek S Pugh, London: Penguin Books, 1995

Bargaining across borders: how to negotiate business successfully anywhere in the world, Dean Allen Foster, New York: McGraw Hill, 1995

Debrett's guide to business etiquette: the complete book of modern business practice and etiquette, Nicholas Yapp, London: Headline, 1994

Dos and taboos around the world, 3rd ed, Roger E Axtell, New York: John Wiley, 1993

We Europeans, 4th ed, Richard Hill, Brussels: Europublications, 1993

The dos and taboos of international trade: a small business primer, Roger E Axtell, New York: John Wiley, 1989

Thought starters

- What treatment by a foreigner would embarrass or annoy you?
- What stereotypes come into your mind when you think of the foreigners you will be meeting? Do they have sound bases or should you discuss them?
- 'Visitors' may, in some contexts, be a more appropriate description than 'foreigners'.

Further *Business Checklists* titles from Hodder & Stoughton and the Institute of Management all at £8.99

0 340 74292 5	Information & Financial Management	❐
0 340 74290 9	Marketing & Strategy	❐
0 340 74291 7	Operations & Quality Management	❐
0 340 74288 7	People Management	❐
0 340 74294 1	Personal Effectiveness & Career Development	❐
0 340 74289 5	Personnel Policies, Training & Development	❐

All Hodder & Stoughton books are available from your local bookshop or can be ordered direct from the publisher. Just tick the titles you want and fill in the form below. Prices and availability subject to change without notice.

To: Hodder & Stoughton Ltd, Cash Sales Department, Bookpoint, 78 Milton Park, Abingdon, Oxon OX14 4TD. If you have a credit card you may order by telephone – 01235 400414
                    fax – 01235 400454
E-mail address: orders@bookpoint.co.uk

Please enclose a cheque or postal order made payable to Bookpoint Ltd to the value of the cover price and allow the following for postage and packaging:

UK & BFPO: £4.30 for one book; £6.30 for two books; £8.30 for three books.

OVERSEAS & EIRE: £4.80 for one book; £7.10 for 2 or 3 books (surface mail).

Name: ....

Address: ....

....

....

If you would prefer to pay by credit card, please complete:

Please debit my Visa/Mastercard/Diner's Card/American Express (delete as appropriate) card no:

❐ ❐ ❐ ❐ ❐ ❐ ❐ ❐ ❐ ❐ ❐ ❐ ❐ ❐ ❐ ❐

Signature .... Expiry date ....